Original Title: 101 Strange But True Surf Facts

© 101 Strange But True Surf Facts, Carlos
Martínez Cerdá and Víctor Martínez Cerdá, 2023

Authors: Víctor Martínez Cerdá and Carlos
Martínez Cerdá (V&C Brothers)

© Cover and illustrations: V&C Brothers

Layout and design: V&C Brothers

101

STRANGE BUT TRUE

SURF FACTS

INCREDIBLE AND SURPRISING FACTS

1

The figure of 7.3 trillion euros.

This figure represents the estimated annual value generated by the global surfing industry.

The information is provided by Statistic Brain and reflects the wide range of activities and sectors related to surfing, including the manufacturing and sale of surfboards, equipment and accessories, specialized clothing and footwear, surf-related tourism services, competitions and events, among others.

Furthermore, it is mentioned that this figure is expected to increase significantly in the following years.

This suggests a forecasted growth for the surfing industry in the short term.

This increase could be attributed to various factors, such as the growing popularity of surfing as a recreational and sporting activity, the rise in surf-related tourism, and the expansion of markets and demand for surf-related products and services.

It is important to note that the surfing industry not only has a direct economic impact but can also have positive effects on tourism, local job creation, the promotion of coastal destinations, and environmental conservation.

2

**35 million is the estimated number of people
who practice surfing worldwide.**

This figure is provided by Ponting/O'Brien and is based
on data collected from 162 countries.

It is worth noting that the number of surfers has
experienced significant growth over the years.

In 2002, it was estimated that there were only 10
million surfers worldwide, indicating an increase of
approximately one million new practitioners per year.

Regarding regional distribution, it is mentioned that the
Americas lead with 13.5 million surfers.

This suggests that America has a large base of surfing
enthusiasts and practitioners.

On the other hand, Europe is estimated to have 4.5
million surfers, indicating a significant presence on the
continent.

It is important to highlight that surfing has gained
popularity worldwide due to various factors, such as
increased beach accessibility, the promotion of surf
tourism, media coverage of competitions and events,
and the influence of surf culture in music, film, and
fashion.

3

$5.3 million is the figure for professional surfer John John Florence's total earnings in the year 2018.

John John Florence is recognized as one of the most successful and talented professional surfers in the world.

These earnings of $5.3 million encompass a variety of income sources related to his surfing career.

This may include cash prizes earned through competitions and events, royalties from sponsorship agreements, and contracts with various brands and companies.

It is important to note that professional surfers, like John John Florence, have the opportunity to earn significant income through a combination of cash prizes in competitions, sponsorships, and marketing agreements.

The success and status of a surfer, as well as their performance in the professional circuit, can influence the amount of income they can generate.

John John Florence, in particular, has managed to stand out in the surfing scene and has achieved significant accomplishments and titles throughout his career.

His skill and popularity have contributed to his ability to secure lucrative sponsorship contracts and earn considerable earnings.

It is important to consider that the earnings of professional surfers can vary significantly from year to year, and there are also other successful surfers who may have similar or even higher earnings figures at different times.

4

The year 1928 marks an important milestone in the history of surfing as the Pacific Coast Surfriding Championship was held, considered the first documented surfing competition.

The event took place in Corona del Mar, California, United States, and was organized by the local surf club, which had twelve members.

The 1928 Pacific Coast Surfriding Championship was a pioneering event in the development of surfing as a competitive sport.

While surf competitions had been held previously in Hawaii, this championship in California marked a crucial moment in popularizing surfing as an organized sport.

It is worth noting that surfing as a sport and culture originated in the Hawaiian islands, where it was an integral part of society and local tradition for centuries before spreading to California and other parts of the world.

However, it was in California where the first recorded and documented surf championships began to be organized.

As for Europe, the first major surf championship was held in Lacanau, France, in 1979, known as the Lacanau Pro.

This event marked the beginning of competitive surfing in Europe and helped boost the popularity of the sport in the region.

Since then, both the Pacific Coast Surfriding Championship and the Lacanau Pro have laid the foundation for the growth and evolution of surfing as a competitive sport in different parts of the world.

5

**1738 feet (approximately 530 meters) is the height
of the largest wave ever recorded.**

This event occurred in Lituya Bay, Alaska, in 1958, as a result of a magnitude 7.8 earthquake that triggered a mega-tsunami.

On July 9, 1958, a strong earthquake shook the region of Lituya Bay.

The earthquake was so powerful that it caused a massive landslide on Mount Lituya, located near the bay.

This landslide fell into the water and generated a huge wave that propagated through Lituya Bay.

This gigantic wave reached extraordinary heights, estimated at 1738 feet (approximately 530 meters).

It was an unusually large and record-breaking wave that resulted in significant devastation in the surrounding area.

It is important to note that this particular wave is considered an extremely exceptional event.

Waves of this magnitude are extremely rare and form under very specific circumstances, such as in the case of massive landslides or large-scale seismic events.

The mega-tsunami resulting from the earthquake and landslide in Lituya Bay had a significant impact on the area, causing extensive damage and loss of human lives.

6

27.81 meters is the size of the largest wave ever recorded to date in Spanish waters.

This record-breaking wave, measured from trough to crest, was recorded by the Deep-Water Buoys Network of Puertos del Estado in January 2014 at Cabo Vilán, located in A Coruña, Galicia.

The Deep-Water Buoys Network of Puertos del Estado is a network of ocean monitoring devices used to measure maritime and oceanographic conditions in Spanish waters.

These buoys are equipped with sensors and technology to collect accurate data about the state of the sea, including wave size and height.

The recording of a 27.81-meter wave at Cabo Vilán in January 2014 indicates an exceptional and large-scale event.

The specific weather and oceanographic conditions at that time contributed to the formation of this gigantic wave.

It is important to highlight that measuring the size of a wave can be a complex process and depends on various factors, including location, measurement method used, and the specific definition of wave size (such as measuring from trough to crest or from face to crest).

Surfing in Spain boasts numerous renowned areas internationally recognized for the quality of their waves, such as the northern coast of Spain, where some of the most famous and challenging spots for surfers are found.

7

24.38 meters is the record for the largest wave ever surfed, established by Brazilian surfer Rodrigo Koxa.

This achievement took place at Praia do Norte, Nazaré, Portugal, on November 8, 2017, and earned Koxa the recognition from the Guinness World Records.

Praia do Norte in Nazaré is known for having some of the biggest and most challenging waves in the world due to its unique geographical formation and the presence of large ocean currents.

The conditions in Nazaré attract professional surfers and adventurous individuals seeking high thrills and extreme challenges.

This feat requires a combination of skill, bravery, and technical knowledge to handle and ride a wave of such magnitude.

Additionally, in the women's category, there is a debate about the biggest wave surfed by a woman.

Two prominent names in this discussion are Justine Dupont and Maya Gabeira.

Justine Dupont surfed a wave in November 2019, and Maya Gabeira achieved a similar feat in October 2018.

Both waves are estimated to be around 20.72 meters (68 feet).

These achievements in surfing showcase the dedication and courage of elite surfers who seek to push the boundaries and face extreme conditions in the ocean.

8

The number 66 represents the record for the most people riding a single surfboard to date.

This historic feat took place in Huntington Beach, California, United States, in June 2015.

In this event, a group of 66 individuals joined forces to ride a single surfboard.

The board used for this endeavor measured 12 meters in length and weighed 589 kilograms.

It was a coordinated and challenging effort that required careful planning and the collaboration of all participants.

This type of record is a testament to the creativity, dedication, and passion of the individuals involved in the world of surfing.

In addition to enjoying the sport individually, this achievement demonstrates surfers' ability to come together and overcome collective challenges.

Huntington Beach, also known as Surf City USA, is famous for its surfing culture and history.

It is an iconic destination for surfers and has been the venue for numerous events and competitions over the years.

9

The study conducted by the Sports Performance Research Institute of New Zealand (SPRINZ) reveals that during a 20-minute competition heat, surfers spend approximately 8% of the time standing on the surfboard.

This means that, on average, surfers are standing and riding waves for a relatively low percentage of time compared to other activities such as paddling and waiting.

According to the study, surfers spend around 54% of the time paddling, which involves using their arms to move through the water and position themselves properly to catch waves.

This is an essential component of surfing and requires significant physical effort. Additionally, it was found that surfers spend approximately 28% of the time sitting on the surfboard waiting.

This refers to the time when surfers are in the water but not actively paddling or riding waves.

During this time, surfers search for the best waves, assess the conditions, and patiently wait for opportunities to catch quality waves.

Overall, during a freesurf session, a mid-level surfer may spend more time standing on the surfboard compared to a competition, as the main focus is to enjoy and practice surfing without the pressure of scoring or limited time.

However, the amount of time spent paddling and waiting will depend on the ocean conditions, location, and the surfer's personal preferences.

Each freesurf session is unique and can vary widely in terms of the amount of time a surfer spends standing, paddling, or waiting. In the end, the main goal is to enjoy surfing and make the most of every opportunity in the water.

10

**The figure of 3.55 hours represents the longest
time someone has surfed a wave.**

This record was set by Panamanian surfer Gary Saavedra in 2011 at
Lake Gatun, located on the Pacific side of the Panama Canal.

Gary Saavedra achieved this record by practicing wake-surfing, a
modality in which a boat is used to generate a non-static wave on
which the surfer glides.

In this case, the boat created a wave on Lake Gatun, allowing
Saavedra to surf for an impressive time of 3.55 hours.

During his feat, Gary Saavedra covered a total distance of 41.3
miles (66.46 kilometers) on the wave generated in Lake Gatun.

This achievement required a high level of physical and mental
endurance, as well as advanced surfing skills to maintain balance
and make the most of the wave's conditions.

Lake Gatun is an important body of water in Panama, formed as
part of the Panama Canal.

The location and characteristics of the lake provided the perfect
opportunity for Saavedra to establish this world record.

The fact that this record was set using a wave generated by a non-
static boat highlights the diversity and creativity in the world of
surfing.

While most surfers focus on natural ocean waves, wake-surfing
and other forms of boat-propelled surfing offer unique and
exciting opportunities to experiment with the sport.

11

Agatha Christie, the famous British writer of mystery novels, was one of the early English women to practice surfing.

This fact occurred in the 1920s, which is notable considering that surfing was not as popular or widespread at that time as it is today.

In 1924, Agatha Christie accompanied her husband on a trip through the British Empire, visiting countries such as New Zealand, South Africa, and Hawaii.

During her stay in Hawaii, she had the opportunity to try surfing and ride a wave.

In her diary, Agatha Christie left an account of her surfing experience, mentioning that there may be some harm in falling headfirst onto the sand, but overall, she considered the sport to be simple and quite fun.

It is interesting to note that Agatha Christie, known for her prowess in writing and her talent for creating intriguing stories, also had the courage and curiosity to venture into the world of surfing at a time when it was uncommon for women, especially for a woman of her social position.

Agatha Christie's involvement in surfing is not only a curious fact but also a reminder of the diversity of interests and experiences that people can have, even those who excel in other fields.

12

The famous music group The Beach Boys based much of their career and music on the theme of surfing.

Their iconic songs like "Surfin' U.S.A.," "Surfer Girl," and "Good Vibrations" captured the essence and culture of surfing in the 1960s.

However, despite their strong connection to surfing in their music, it is said that none of the members of The Beach Boys had actual surfing skills or practiced the sport itself.

Although the band identified with and strongly associated themselves with surf culture, they were primarily focused on music and portraying the image of surfing rather than being active surfers.

Their focus was more on creating catchy songs and evoking the spirit and lifestyle of surfing through their music.

Over the years, members of the band have clarified in interviews that while they loved the music and surf culture, they were not actual surfers.

Some of them may have had occasional experiences at the beach or hopped on a surfboard now and then, but they were not dedicated surfers.

It is important to note that the success of The Beach Boys was not based on their personal surfing experience but on their musical talent, distinctive vocal style, and ability to capture the essence of the era and surf culture through their music.

Despite not being real-life surfers, The Beach Boys' legacy in music and their association with surfing made them one of the most influential groups of the time and an important part of the history of the surf rock genre.

13

The cutback is one of the most popular and preferred maneuvers by surfers.

It involves making a turn or redirecting in the opposite direction on the wave, allowing the surfer to regain the critical part of the wave when they are too far forward.

This maneuver is especially useful when the surfer is in the most critical part of the wave and needs to readjust their position to continue their ride and make the most of the wave's energy.

By performing a cutback, the surfer slows down and executes a turn towards the opposite side of the original direction, allowing them to return to the wave face and maintain speed and fluidity in their ride.

The cutback is performed through a shift in weight and controlled pressure on the edges of the surfboard.

The surfer utilizes their skill and technique to execute the turn smoothly and fluidly, harnessing the energy of the wave while maintaining control.

This maneuver is highly valued by surfers due to its spectacular nature and its ability to maintain rhythm and speed in the wave ride.

Additionally, the cutback allows surfers to express their personal style and creativity by performing different variations and combinations of turns.

According to a survey conducted among surfers, the cutback is considered one of the favorite moves by the majority of them.

Its popularity lies in the sense of control and fluidity it provides while surfing, as well as its visual impact and the technical skill required to execute it correctly.

14

Tsunamis cannot be surfed.

Unlike waves generated by wind or normal swells, tsunamis are large, high-energy ocean waves that originate from disturbances on the seafloor, typically caused by underwater earthquakes, volcanic eruptions, or submarine landslides.

Tsunamis are characterized by their extremely high speed and size.

These waves can travel at speeds of up to several hundred kilometers per hour, making them uncontrollable and dangerous for anyone attempting to surf them.

Furthermore, the characteristics of tsunamis make them very different from ideal waves for surfing.

Tsunamis do not have a defined shape or predictable trajectory and are often a series of waves with irregular intervals.

These waves can also contain large amounts of debris and sediment, making them even more dangerous and unpredictable.

Due to the immense energy and force possessed by tsunamis, their impact on the coast can be devastating and pose a serious threat to human life and coastal infrastructure.

15

The use of wax on surfboards as a way to increase grip and prevent slipping is very common in the practice of surfing.

Although the discovery of this use of wax cannot be attributed exclusively to Alfred Gallant, his observation and application in the context of surfing have been significant.

Wax is a waxy and slippery substance obtained from petroleum.

Its use on surfboards dates back decades when surfers began seeking ways to improve the grip of their feet on the board's surface.

Prior to the application of wax, surfboards used to have a smooth and polished surface, making it difficult to maintain balance and control on the board.

Alfred Gallant, upon observing the non-slip effects of wax on the floor, decided to try it on his surfboard.

Noticing that wax provided better grip and prevented slipping, its use became popular within the surfing community.

Wax is applied to the surface of the surfboard, primarily in the area where the surfer's feet are placed.

Wax is rubbed onto the board in the form of bars or blocks, creating a layer of sticky wax.

This layer of wax creates a rough texture that allows the surfer's feet to better adhere to the board, providing greater control and stability during surfing.

It is important to note that the amount and quality of wax used can vary according to each surfer's individual preferences and water and temperature conditions.

Some surfers prefer a thicker layer of wax for a stronger grip, while others may prefer a thinner layer for increased glide.

16

The origin of surfing is a debated topic, and there are different theories regarding it.

While Hawaii is widely recognized as the place where surfing developed and became part of its culture, there is also evidence of a similar sport being practiced in other parts of the world, such as Peru.

In Peru, ceramic pieces depicting human figures on boards riding waves have been found, indicating the existence of an ancient tradition of water sliding.

These depictions date back to before the arrival of Europeans to America and suggest that ancient Peruvians were already practicing some form of surfing.

However, it is important to highlight that surfing as we know it today, with the use of modern surfboards, specific techniques, and a culture rooted around the sport, developed and became popular in Hawaii.

During the 18th and 19th centuries, the influence of European colonizers in Hawaii led to the prohibition of many traditional activities, including surfing.

This prohibition had a negative impact on the practice of surfing in Hawaii and resulted in a decline in its popularity.

The resurgence of surfing in the 20th century is largely attributed to Duke Kahanamoku, a Hawaiian Olympic swimming champion born in 1890.

Duke Kahanamoku, also known as the "Big Kahuna," played a key role in promoting and spreading surfing in Hawaii and beyond.

Duke is considered the inventor of modern surfing due to his influence in popularizing the sport and his ability to craft improvised surfboards.

17

The story of Donald Detlof as a surfboard collector is fascinating.

He is considered one of the greatest surfboard collectors in the world, with an impressive collection of over 800 boards of different styles, sizes, and constructions.

Detlof's collection was housed in his own home in Hawaii for many years. What started as a small hobby turned into a passion and an obsession to preserve surfboards and prevent them from being destroyed.

Locals soon recognized his dedication and began leaving their unused boards at his doorstep, knowing that he would take care of them and add them to his collection.

One interesting story is that Detlof decided to use the surfboards to build a fence around his house.

This not only allowed him to display his impressive collection but also became a unique way to protect his property.

The surfboard fence has become an iconic attraction in Hawaii and has caught the attention of surf enthusiasts from around the world.

Donald Detlof's dedication and passion for preserving and collecting surfboards have made him a prominent figure in the surfing community.

His collection is not only impressive in size but also represents the history and evolution of surfing over the years.

It is a testament to his love for the sport and his desire to keep the surf culture alive.

18

Henry P. Douglas was a vice admiral and director of the Meteorological Service of the British Navy in 1917.

During his time in service, he created a scale for classifying the sea based on wave size.

This scale, known as the "Douglas Scale," is still used today to provide maritime indications of sea conditions, swells, and tides.

The Douglas Scale classifies different states of the sea into 10 degrees, taking into account wave size.

It starts at degree 0, which represents a calm sea with virtually no waves, and increases up to degree 9, indicating an extremely rough sea with very large and dangerous waves.

Degree 10 represents an extreme situation with giant waves and extremely hazardous conditions.

It is important to note that in the practice of surfing, different scales are used to measure wave intensity.

In addition to the Douglas Scale, the Beaufort Scale is also taken into consideration.

The Beaufort Scale focuses on wind intensity and is based on sea state, wind force, and wave characteristics.

This scale provides a broader description of general sea conditions and is used alongside the Douglas Scale to assess surfing conditions.

Both the Douglas Scale and the Beaufort Scale are important tools for surfers as they allow them to evaluate sea conditions and make informed decisions about when and where to surf, considering wave intensity and wind strength.

19

**Although not as well-known as ocean surfing, river surfing
has gained popularity in recent years.**

It involves taking advantage of certain conditions and specific features of
certain rivers that create surfable waves, known as standing river waves.

These standing river waves form during certain times of the year when the
river flow creates a reverse current that breaks and forms a stationary wave.

Unlike the ocean, where waves move, these waves in rivers remain in a
specific location, providing the opportunity to surf them for an extended
period of time.

Some well-known places for river surfing include:

1. France: It is particularly popular in regions near the Alps, where mountain
snowmelt creates strong currents and waves in rivers.

2. Canada: The Ottawa River is famous for its surfable waves and attracts
surfers from around the world.

3. United States: In Missoula, Montana, the Clark Fork River offers consistent
surfable waves, while other rivers in different parts of the country also provide
opportunities for river surfing.

4. Germany: The Eisbach River in Munich is a well-known destination for river
surfing and features a permanent wave in the city center.

These are just a few examples, but there are more locations worldwide where
river surfing can be practiced.

It is important to note that river surfing presents different challenges and
characteristics compared to ocean surfing, so it is recommended to have
experience in the water and take additional safety precautions when surfing in
these conditions.

If you're passionate about surfing and looking for new experiences, it's
definitely worth giving river surfing a try.

It can be an exciting and unique way to enjoy waves in a different
environment!

20

Dogs are also part of the surfing world and have their own international competition in Huntington Beach, California.

The event is called Surf City Surf Dog and has been organized for several years with the goal of raising funds for animal welfare organizations.

In Surf City Surf Dog, dogs compete in different categories and are evaluated based on their confidence and ability to tackle the waves, as well as their ability to stay on surfboards.

Canine participants showcase their skill and balance while riding the waves, creating a fun and thrilling spectacle for spectators.

The contest has gained popularity and has become a highly anticipated event for both surf and dog enthusiasts.

Participants and their owners strive to train and prepare for the event, demonstrating the close bond and fun that can be shared between humans and their canine companions.

Surf City Surf Dog is not only a fun competition, but it also serves a charitable purpose by raising money for organizations dedicated to animal welfare.

This reflects the importance of promoting care and love for animals while enjoying a sporting activity.

21

Wave Skiing, or skiing on waves, is a sport that combines skiing and surfing in a unique and thrilling way.

Although not as well-known as other water sports, Wave Skiing has existed since the 1970s and has gained popularity in certain places.

Wave Skiing is practiced using a special board called a waveski, which resembles a surfboard but has a seat and foot straps that allow the skier to stay stable while riding the waves.

The waveski also comes with a kayak paddle that the surfer/skier uses to paddle and maneuver in the waves.

Unlike traditional water skiing, where you ski on a flat and smooth surface, Wave Skiing is done in the ocean, taking advantage of waves as a natural ski slope.

Wave Skiing enthusiasts seek out big waves and breakers to experience the thrill of skiing in an aquatic environment.

One of the most famous spots for Wave Skiing is at Pe'ahi, also known as "JAWS," in Hawaii.

Surfer and skier Chuck Patterson has become increasingly popular for his impressive skiing skills on waves using actual skis at this legendary spot.

Wave Skiing is a demanding discipline that requires skill, balance, and water experience.

Practitioners must have knowledge of both skiing and surfing to master this sport and enjoy the exhilarating sensations it offers.

22

**When we're surfing, we face the force and weight
of the water in a very intense way.**

Although falling into the water may seem harmless, the reality is that waves can be extremely powerful and pose a risk to surfers.

When you're surfing and you fall off the board, especially on a big wave, you can experience a sensation of impact similar to being hit by a heavy object.

The force of the water can be overwhelming and feel like 300 cars crashing onto you.

When you're paddling back to the lineup, meaning trying to get back to the area where the waves are breaking, you can encounter a wave coming at you with a lot of force.

This situation can be challenging and dangerous, as you have to face the impact of the wave and overcome it to keep moving forward.

Waves breaking on your face can be particularly impactful and painful.

The water can hit you with considerable force, causing sensations similar to being slapped.

This can result in injuries such as cuts, bruises, or even temporary disorientation underwater.

It's important to remember that surfing is a risky sport and we must be physically and mentally prepared to face the conditions of the ocean.

More experienced surfers learn to anticipate and manage these impacts, developing skills such as duck diving to pass under the waves and avoid direct impact.

The practice of surfing involves accepting certain risks and learning to deal with the force of the water safely.

It's important to be aware of the ocean conditions, know your abilities and limitations, and always respect and adapt to the ever-changing nature of the waves.

23

Calculating the exact weight of a wave can be complicated due to different variables involved.

However, there are estimates and approximate calculations that have been made to get an idea of the weight of waves.

In a Storm Surfers video, it is mentioned that one cubic meter of water in a 10-meter-high wave weighs approximately 1 ton.

This estimate is based on the density of water and provides a reference for the weight of the water contained in a wave of certain dimensions.

If we take, for example, a 10-meter-high wave with a lip of 20 meters, it is estimated to fall with a force of approximately 400 tons.

This calculation takes into account both the height of the wave and its amplitude, considering the total weight of the moving mass of water.

In the case of a more modest-sized wave, such as an average 3-foot-high wave (around 1 meter) with a lip that is 50 centimeters wide and 1.5 meters long, its weight is estimated to be around 500 kilograms.

This figure gives an idea of the impact such a wave could have if it were to fall on someone.

It is important to note that these calculations are approximate and are based on estimations and general measurements.

The actual weight of a wave can vary depending on factors such as the shape of the wave, water density, speed, and force of impact.

Additionally, the weight of a wave is not evenly distributed, as the majority of the weight is concentrated in the lip or crest of the wave.

24

The phenomenon of tides is a natural process that directly affects the practice of surfing and is related to the ebb and flow of seawater.

While tides are almost imperceptible in the Mediterranean, in places like the Atlantic or the Cantabrian Sea, tides play a crucial role in determining the best time for surfing.

Tides are caused by the gravitational attraction exerted by the Sun and the Moon on the bodies of water in the seas and oceans.

This attraction creates a constant movement in the seawater, generating regular cycles of high and low tides.

The movement of tides is a result of the combined gravitational force of the Sun and the Moon, as well as the rotation of the Earth.

The alignment of the Sun, the Moon, and the Earth plays an important role in the amplitude of tides.

During the new moon and full moon phases, when the Sun and the Moon are aligned with the Earth, spring tides occur, which have greater amplitude.

Conversely, during the first quarter and third quarter moon phases, when the Sun and the Moon are at right angles to the Earth, neap tides occur, which have lower amplitude.

It is important to note that tides are not uniform in all coastlines around the world due to geographical conditions and characteristics of the seafloor and coastline.

Therefore, tide charts provide information about the tide level at a specific location and time.

These charts are consulted by surfers and other individuals engaged in ocean-related activities to determine the most suitable times for surfing or other water activities.

Each day, there are approximately two high tides and two low tides, occurring approximately every 6 hours, although the timings can vary daily due to differences in the duration of the lunar and solar cycles.

Therefore, it is necessary to consult tide charts to obtain precise information about tide timings at a specific location.

The choice of the right time for surfing is influenced by the tide level.

Generally, it is preferable to surf at high tide to avoid potential underwater obstacles such as rocks or reefs.

However, there are certain waves that form or are more suitable at low tide, so it is important to know the characteristics of each surf spot and consult with local surfers or experts to obtain accurate information about the best time to surf at each location.

25

Learning to surf offers a wide range of physical, mental, and emotional benefits.

- **Improved physical fitness:** Surfing is a demanding sport that involves the use of many muscle groups. Paddling to catch waves helps strengthen the arms, shoulders, and back, while balance and standing up on the board work the core muscles, legs, and glutes. Additionally, the constant activity in the water contributes to improving cardiovascular endurance and flexibility.

- **Mental and emotional well-being:** Surfing can be a form of moving meditation. Being in the water and connecting with the waves and the natural environment can help reduce stress, calm the mind, and improve mood. The contact with nature and the sense of freedom and escapism that surfing provides can generate a feeling of happiness and fulfillment. Furthermore, the mental challenge of reading the waves and making quick decisions while surfing helps develop concentration and mental sharpness.

- **Connection with nature:** Surfing allows for a deep connection with the ocean and nature in general. Paddling in the middle of the ocean, feeling the power of the waves, and observing the beauty of the marine environment provides a sense of calm and connection with something greater than oneself. This connection with nature can foster a greater appreciation and respect for the environment.

- **Personal growth:** Learning to surf involves facing challenges and overcoming fears. The learning process can be frustrating and requires perseverance and determination. Overcoming obstacles and achieving small breakthroughs in surfing can generate a sense of accomplishment and strengthen self-confidence. Additionally, surfing provides an opportunity to push personal limits, try new things, and step out of the comfort zone, which can be empowering and foster personal growth.

- **Community and social connections:** Surfing is a sport that is practiced in a community. By sharing waves with other surfers, a sense of camaraderie and social connections are formed. Surfing promotes teamwork, companionship, and solidarity. Furthermore, the surfing community is diverse and multicultural, providing an opportunity to meet people from different parts of the world, learn about different cultures, and establish lasting friendships based on a shared passion.

26

The term "Super Set" refers to a set of giant waves breaking in a specific location.

At Praia do Norte in Nazaré, Portugal, the "Super Set" consisted of a series of four massive and dangerous waves.

In a video, filmmaker Pedro Miranda captured this set of waves and subsequently shared it, generating significant attention and dissemination worldwide.

The "Super Set" stood out for featuring four consecutive waves, each being surfed by different surfers.

The first surfer to tackle one of these waves was Axi Muniain, originally from the Basque Country.

Then, Chilean surfer Rafael Tapia rode the second wave of the set.

The third and largest wave was surfed by Brazilian Rodrigo Koxa, who became famous for riding the largest wave ever recorded in Nazaré in 2017.

It is important to note that these giant waves pose a great challenge and danger to surfers.

Surfing in places like Praia do Norte requires exceptional skills, experience, and extensive physical and mental preparation.

27

The "10 lies every surfer has told at some point" are humorous and exaggerated expressions that surfers often use in a joking manner.

Here's a description of each of them:

- **"It used to be different"**: Used to justify a bad day of surfing by attributing the adverse conditions to external factors, such as the tide, too many people in the water, or the absence of dolphins.

- **"Early morning tomorrow!"**: Surfers often plan to wake up early to take advantage of the best surfing conditions, but sometimes it's challenging to get up early, especially after a night of fun.

- **"Just a quick session!"**: When a surfer says this, it usually means they'll be in the water for a long time, enjoying the surf and not in a hurry to get out.

- **"The next one is yours"**: A surf instructor or fellow surfer may offer to give the next good wave to another surfer, but sometimes they may change their mind and paddle for it themselves.

- **"Did you see that massive barrel?"**: Surfers often exaggerate their achievements and talk about epic barrels, even if they haven't actually experienced them.

- **"It's just water!"**: Although surfing is fun, surfers are aware that it also involves risks and challenges, such as big waves, strong currents, or dangerous conditions. However, they often downplay these aspects and say, "It's just water."

- **"I wasn't feeling well"**: Surfers may use this excuse to justify why they didn't go surfing, even if they simply didn't feel like it or were busy with other things.

- **"I'll let you know as soon as I see the surf"**: When someone is eagerly waiting to know the surf conditions, they may promise to notify others as soon as they have the information, but sometimes they forget or simply don't follow through.

- **"Just one more wave and I'm out!"**: Similar to saying "one last beer," surfers often say they're going to leave the water after one more wave, but then they keep surfing because they can't resist the fun.

- **"I didn't see you"**: Due to the concentration and excitement of surfing, surfers may not have noticed someone in the water or they may use this humorous excuse to justify a minor incident.

28

Some tips for holding your breath underwater for longer:

- **Lung capacity training:** Perform breathing exercises and specific training to strengthen your lungs. Breath-holding tables, mentioned earlier, where you alternate periods of apnea, are helpful for increasing lung endurance.

- **Breathing technique:** Learn to breathe efficiently before submerging. Take deep, slow breaths before a dive to properly oxygenate your body.

- **Relaxation and mental control:** Stay calm and relax your mind before and during the dive. Stress can negatively affect your breath-holding ability. Practice relaxation techniques like meditation and visualization to maintain tranquility in challenging situations.

- **Gradual progression:** Gradually increase the time you spend underwater. Don't try to exceed your limits immediately, as it could be dangerous. Gradually extend your apnea times as you feel more comfortable and confident.

- **Maintain physical fitness:** Engage in cardiovascular and endurance exercises to improve your overall physical condition. A well-conditioned body can utilize oxygen more efficiently.

- **Avoid panic:** If you feel uncomfortable or the need to breathe during a dive, stay calm and resurface slowly. Don't force yourself beyond your limits and always prioritize your safety.

The 10 longest waves in the world:

- **The Bono, Indonesia:** This river wave is formed on the Kampar River in Sumatra Island, thanks to the "Tidal Bore" phenomenon. It provides an almost endless wave for surfers.

- **Punta Roca, El Salvador:** It is a right-hand wave with a long ride, offering endless rides on its crest.

- **Chicama, Peru:** Considered the longest left-hand wave in the world, it can be surfed for over 2 km under the right conditions. It has been the setting for world records in distance traveled, time, and maneuvers on a single wave.

- **Skeleton Bay, Namibia:** This spot is known for its long and hollow left-hand waves, immortalized in images of professional surfers like Cory López.

- **Raglan, New Zealand:** It is a very popular left-hand wave in New Zealand, especially known for its long ride.

- **Superbank, Australia:** This is a long and nearly perfect wave that stretches from Snapper Beach to the Kirra spot. It is highly recommended for surfers from all over the world.

- **Pavones, Costa Rica:** Under suitable conditions, this incredible left-hand wave offers an impressive ride, allowing surfers to enjoy the same wave for several minutes.

- **Qiantang River, China:** This river wave is formed by the natural phenomenon known as the "Tidal Bore," creating a wave called "The Silver Dragon." It is an unforgettable experience for surfers who enjoy a long ride on the same wave.

- **Pororoca, Brazil:** Similar to the Qiantang River wave, it forms in the Amazon and travels with great force through part of the river's estuary. The name "Pororoca" means "great roar," describing the sound and sensation produced by this endless wave.

- **Jeffreys Bay, South Africa:** It is famous for being one of the longest and most perfect right-hand waves in the world, thanks to its long ride and quality shape. It is a paradise for surfers seeking an exceptional experience.

30

"The Tool" is an essential tool for any surfer.

It is a kind of Swiss army knife designed specifically to facilitate the practice of surfing.

This multifunctional tool usually includes a fin key, Allen keys of different sizes to adjust the surfboard's screws, a can opener, a screwdriver, an air valve key, and possibly other useful functions.

With "The Tool," surfers can make quick repairs and adjustments to their equipment without the need to carry multiple separate tools.

The "Surf Lock" is another useful accessory for surfers.

Often, when surfers go out to surf, they need to find a secure place to store their car keys while they are in the water.

It is common to hide keys under the car or wrap them in a towel, but this is not always safe and can be easily discovered by potential thieves.

The Surf Lock solves this problem by providing a secure storage system for car keys.

It consists of a waterproof and shockproof box where the car key can be placed.

To access the key, the surfer must choose a numerical combination and anchor the Surf Lock in a secure location on the car, such as the wheel or trailer hitch.

This provides peace of mind and security during surf sessions, as the keys are effectively protected.

31

When it comes to transporting a surfboard, there are a variety of gadgets designed to make it easier and more convenient.

- **Seat Rack:** It is an alternative to traditional roof racks for transporting surfboards in a car. This system consists of an internal board carrier that is placed on the rear seat of the vehicle. It provides comfort and safety when transporting boards inside the car, avoiding the use of external roof racks.

- **Surfboard Carrier:** It is a device specifically designed to carry surfboards, especially SUP or longboards, more easily. It eliminates the need to carry the board under the arm, which can be uncomfortable and tiring. This type of gadget adjusts around the body and provides a secure way to carry the board while walking to or from the beach.

- **Magnetic Rack:** It is a magnetic roof rack designed to transport surfboards on the car's roof. This Spanish invention uses strong magnets to securely attach the surfboard to the vehicle's roof, without the need for additional straps or tie-downs. It provides a simple and quick way to secure the board during surf trips.

- **Wheel Rack:** It is a type of rack specifically designed to transport surfboards on a bicycle. There are different models available on the market, but generally, it is a trailer or support that attaches to the bicycle and allows for independent board transportation. It is especially useful for transporting longboards, as it avoids the difficulty of balancing and holding the board while pedaling.

32

In the water, there are various devices and equipment that can enhance the experience and safety of surfers.

- **Shark Shield:** It is a device designed to deter sharks and reduce the risk of shark attacks. It is placed on the surfboard's traction pad and emits an electric field that interacts with the jelly-filled ampullae of Lorenzini present in shark snouts, causing spasms and driving them away. This device is mainly used in areas where shark attacks are more frequent, such as Australia and South Africa.

- **Lume Cube:** It is a small light cube that can be used both in and out of the water. This device emits a powerful light and can be submerged in water. It is ideal for illuminating underwater shots during surf sessions and can also be used as a flashlight or connected to action cameras like GoPro, drones, or video cameras.

- **GoPro:** GoPro is a popular brand of action cameras among surfers. These cameras are waterproof and can be used to capture high-quality photos and videos during surf sessions. The upcoming model, GoPro Hero 5, promises features such as GPS location system, voice control, rear touch screen, and image stabilization, making it an attractive device for surf enthusiasts who want to document their experiences.

33

**After surfing, there are some gadgets
and tools that can be useful.**

- **Portable Shower:** It is a device that allows you to rinse off and freshen up after getting out of the water. It is especially useful when you don't have access to a shower near the surf spot. There are two common formats: manual portable showers, which are placed on the car roof and heated by the sun, and electric portable showers, which are connected to the car's cigarette lighter. These showers allow you to rinse off accumulated sand and cool down after your surf session.

- **Wetsuit Dryer:** After surfing, it is important to properly dry your wetsuit to avoid unpleasant odors and extend its lifespan. Hanging the wetsuit in the sun is not the best option, as it can accelerate neoprene wear and tear.

Instead, there are some alternatives.

For example, the outdoor drying hanger Go Dry Hanger provides ventilation and allows the wetsuit to dry more efficiently.

Another option is the electric fan hanger HangAir, which provides a constant airflow to dry the wetsuit.

There is also the option of Blawsome, a Spanish-made device that dries and disinfects the wetsuit.

34

Ryan Burch is an American surfer known for his unique style and innovative approach to surfboard design.

Born in California, Burch has become an influential figure in the surfing community due to his creative and unconventional approach.

At the age of 24, Burch has traveled around the world in search of waves and has developed his own line of homemade foam surfboards in a variety of shapes and sizes.

His boards often feature asymmetrical designs, meaning the front and back of the board have different shapes.

This asymmetrical approach challenges traditional conventions of surfboard design and showcases Burch's innovative mindset.

In addition to his focus on design, Ryan Burch is known for his skill in the water.

His surfing level is highly regarded, and he has been praised for his smooth style and ability to perform creative and unconventional maneuvers on waves.

He has been part of the creative team in surf films like "Migrations," where he has showcased his out-of-the-box thinking.

Ryan Burch stands out in a generation of surfers who are often obsessed with technology and social media, and he represents a countercultural mindset by challenging the status quo and seeking new forms of expression in surfing.

He is considered a source of inspiration and creativity for those looking to explore new boundaries in the sport.

35

George Greenough is a legendary figure in the surfing world known for his eccentric genius and innovative approach to photography, surfboard design, and invention.

Although he rose to fame in the 1960s, his creativity and brilliance continue to stand out to this day.

Greenough is nicknamed the "Barefoot Genius" due to his preference for going shoeless in his everyday life.

This quirk reflects his challenging approach and rebellious spirit in a revolutionary and countercultural era.

One of the highlights of Greenough's contribution to surfing is his groundbreaking photography technique.

He pioneered the use of an underwater camera mounted on his surfboard, allowing him to capture unique and immersive images from inside the waves.

His photographs and films, such as "The Innermost Limits of Pure Fun," have been acclaimed for their artistic approach and ability to convey the surfing experience in a new and exciting way.

In addition to photography, Greenough is also known for his visionary surfboard designs.

He was one of the first to experiment with unconventional shapes and materials, such as the use of flexible fins and twin-fin boards.

His revolutionary designs influenced the evolution of surfboards and have left a lasting impact on the sport.

But Greenough's creativity is not limited to surfing.

He is also an inventor and has created a variety of ingenious gadgets, including wind generators and a dolphin-shaped camera housing for his dolphin-themed film project.

Throughout the years, Greenough has maintained his eccentric lifestyle and continued to pursue creative projects that challenge conventions.

His genius and unconventional approach make him a unique and revered figure in the surfing community.

36

Paul Fisher is a former WQS (World Qualifying Series) surfer from the Gold Coast who has gained recognition for his blog, videos on followthefish.tv, and his career as a DJ.

He is known for his peculiar style and extravagant personality.

Fisher has earned a reputation for his rude and lascivious behavior, as well as his distinctive and psychotic laughter.

He is a quirky character who seems to go beyond shame and is unafraid to be bold and provocative.

One of Fisher's distinguishing features is his sexualized approach to the world of surfing.

He has conducted unusual interviews, such as the time he interviewed Kelly Slater using a microphone shaped like a dildo.

Additionally, he has been known to surf famous waves using a custom surfboard shaped like a penis.

These provocative and controversial actions have generated attention and debate within the surfing community.

Fisher's sexualized and provocative approach may not be to everyone's taste and can be polarizing.

However, it is precisely his uniqueness and ability to stand out in an increasingly standardized surfing world that has brought him notoriety and followers.

In addition to his online and surfing world presence, Fisher has ventured into music as a DJ.

His musical style reflects his eccentric personality, and he has performed at surfing-related events and festivals.

37

Matt Wilkinson is a professional surfer who has made his mark in the surfing world with his unique style and passion for design.

Although he has found success in competitions and has stood out on the world circuit, his unconventional personality and approach have made him a distinctive figure in the sport.

Wilkinson gained recognition in the Fiji Pro by reaching the final and improving his position in the world rankings.

As his career has progressed, he has taken a more professional approach and has strived to improve his performance in the water.

In addition to his surfing talent, Wilkinson has showcased his passion for design.

He began showcasing his creativity through his blog called Out 2 Brunch, where he shared his designs for custom wetsuits.

He has also created special designs for the World Surf League (WSL) awards.

His unique style and taste for design have given him a distinctive identity both in and out of the water.

Wilkinson's surfing reflects his creativity and individual style.

His approach in the water is highlighted by his fluidity, his handling of wave sections, and his ability to perform original and surprising maneuvers.

He is recognized for his ability to generate speed and his unconventional approach to surfing.

38

Ross Clarke-Jones is an Australian surfer known for his adventurous lifestyle and bravery in the water.

Born on June 6, 1966, Clarke-Jones has made a lasting impact in the surfing world with his daring feats and near-death experiences.

Throughout his career, Clarke-Jones has constantly pushed the limits of surfing and sought out extreme waves in some of the most dangerous locations in the world.

A notable example is his surfing in the piranha-infested Amazon River, a feat that few surfers would dare to attempt.

Furthermore, Clarke-Jones has been the only Australian surfer invited to the prestigious Quiksilver In Memory Of Eddie Aikau competition held at Waimea Bay, Hawaii.

In 2001, he achieved a milestone by becoming the first non-Hawaiian to win the event, showcasing his skill and courage in Hawaii's big waves.

His unusually frenetic lifestyle and near-death experiences have contributed to his reputation as a fearless and bold surfer.

Clarke-Jones has lived a life filled with thrills and adventures, constantly pushing the limits of surfing and defying the norm.

39

Mason Ho is a Hawaiian surfer known for his unique style, extravagant personality, and ability to surf all kinds of waves.

His unconventional approach and refreshing vision of surfing and life in general have made him one of the most famous and beloved surfers today.

Ho has showcased his surfing prowess by taking on challenging and dangerous waves, such as those at Pipeline in Hawaii.

His ability to read and capitalize on wave conditions has led to impressive maneuvers and captured the attention of surf fans worldwide.

However, what truly sets Mason Ho apart is his unique personality and outlook on life.

In interviews and videos, he comes across as a fun-loving, authentic individual filled with energy.

He speaks unfiltered, and his expression style can sometimes be incomprehensible, but it always proves entertaining and refreshing.

In addition to his skills in the water, Mason Ho is also known for his love of small and unconventional waves.

He enjoys exploring different spots and experimenting with uncommon surfboards and styles.

His carefree attitude and playful approach to surfing have made him a role model for those seeking to enjoy and have fun in the water regardless of wave size.

40

Derek Hynd is a prominent Australian surfer known for his unique surfing style and innovative approach to the sport.

Throughout his career, he has made a significant impact on the world of surfing, both in and out of the water.

In the early 1980s, Derek Hynd managed to rank among the top ten surfers in the world, despite losing an eye in a surfing accident.

This obstacle didn't deter him, and he continued to challenge himself and overcome adversity.

In addition to his surfing ability, Hynd has dabbled in various roles within the surf industry.

He has been a coach, publicist, journalist, and collaborative orchestra performer.

His unique perspective and unconventional thinking have been a constant source of influence and originality in the world of surfing.

One of Derek Hynd's standout moments was when he became the first surfer to enter the water at J-Bay after Mick Fanning's infamous shark attack during a competition.

His courage and determination showcased his approach to challenging situations and his deep connection with the ocean.

Hynd has also been a pioneer in the development and promotion of new forms of surfing.

He played a key role in the launch of Fish surfboards, a revolutionary design that has gained popularity in the surf community.

Additionally, he has been involved in the finless surfing movement, which explores surfing without fins on modified surfboards.

His passion for experimentation and innovation has led to new ideas and approaches in surfing.

41

Life hacks, or tips and techniques to make life easier, are used to perform daily tasks more efficiently and conveniently.

In the context of surfing, there are specific life hacks that can help surfers tackle certain challenges or enhance their experience in the water.

- To make putting on a wetsuit easier, it is suggested to put plastic bags on your feet before wearing it. This allows the wetsuit to slide on more easily.

- Using a plastic doormat to remove the wetsuit on top of it is recommended. This way, you avoid getting sand and water in your car.

- For a quick post-surf shower, it is suggested to fill a used detergent bottle with hot water and poke some holes in the cap. This functions as a portable personal shower.

- Instead of waiting for someone to dig for keys under the car wheels, using a waterproof key pouch is suggested to keep the keys secure while surfing.

- Duct tape can be handy for repairing cuts in the wetsuit or making small fixes on the surfboard. Make sure it doesn't trap water inside.

- To have a warm towel after coming out of the water, it is suggested to wrap it in a hot water bottle before going surfing. This way, the towel will be warm and comforting upon return.

- To remove excess wax from the surfboard, it is recommended to take a pair of old stockings, fill them with flour, and rub the resulting bag on the board. The flour acts as a kind of beanbag to remove the wax.

42

Surfing safely is essential for enjoying a good session in the water.

Here are some tips:

- **Study the spot before entering:** Before getting in the water, it's important to familiarize yourself with the conditions of the spot. Observe the waves, currents, and number of people in the water to ensure they align with your skill level.

- **Stretch and warm up on the beach:** Before entering the water, take some time to stretch and warm up your muscles. This will help prevent injuries and allow you to surf more efficiently.

- **Check your equipment:** Before each surf session, make sure your equipment is in good condition. Ensure your board, leash, wetsuit, and other accessories are in optimal condition. This will help you avoid issues and maintain your safety in the water.

- **Respect priorities:** It's important to respect the rules of priority in surfing. Learn and abide by the order for catching waves. Generally, the surfer closest to the breaking point of the wave has priority. Avoid paddling into a wave that someone is already riding, as this can lead to accidents.

- **Know your limits:** Be honest with yourself and recognize your own abilities and limitations. Don't push yourself in conditions that are beyond your level of experience. Ensure you have the proper physical condition for the surf session and don't exhaust yourself, as this can impede your ability to exit the water.

- **Don't release your board:** Always maintain control over your surfboard. Letting it go can be dangerous, as it can strike other surfers in the water. Make sure to use the leash correctly to prevent the board from getting away from you.

- **Paddle back out with awareness:** If you need to return to the lineup where waves are being caught, do so safely and respectfully. Avoid interfering with surfers who are riding waves and find a route that takes you away from the most crowded areas.

43

When choosing a surfboard, it's important to consider several factors to find the right board that suits your needs and skill level.

Here are some tips:

- **Identify your skill level:** Determine whether you are a beginner, intermediate, or experienced surfer. This will help you select a board that matches your skill level in the water.

- **Consider the type of waves you'll be surfing:** Think about the conditions of the spot where you'll usually surf. If the waves are small and mellow, opting for a longboard or a larger board may be suitable. If the waves are bigger and faster, you might need a shorter and more maneuverable board.

- **Consult with experts or professionals:** If you have doubts about what type of board is best for you, seek advice from more experienced surfers or visit a specialized surf shop. They can guide you and recommend the most suitable board based on your needs.

- **Consider the size and volume of the board:** The size and volume of the board will affect its buoyancy and stability in the water. Beginners often benefit from larger boards with higher volume as they provide more stability and easier paddling. More advanced surfers can opt for smaller, more maneuverable boards.

- **Try different types of boards:** If possible, try out different board models before making a purchase. By renting or borrowing a surfboard, you can get a clearer idea of how it feels and suits your surfing style.

- **Consider the board's material:** Surfboards can be made from various materials, such as foam or resin. Softboards, like the ones offered by Kürüf, are ideal for beginners as they provide greater buoyancy, stability, and safety in the water.

44

Tips for beginner surfers before getting in the water:

- **Don't learn to surf alone:** It's crucial to have the supervision and guidance of someone experienced when learning to surf. An experienced friend or a surf instructor can teach you the proper techniques and provide important safety advice.

- **Choose a good teacher:** If you decide to take surf lessons, research the available instructors. Look for professionals with experience and positive reviews. A good teacher will not only teach you how to surf but also motivate you and help you fall in love with the sport.

- **Do light exercises:** Before getting in the water, it's recommended to do warm-up exercises to prepare your muscles and tendons. Stretching will help prevent muscle cramps and improve blood circulation, getting you ready for the physical activity of surfing.

- **Choose a beginner-friendly beach:** It's important to select a beach that is suitable for beginner surfers. Look for places with gentle and consistent waves, where it's easier to learn and improve your skills. Consult local guides or gather information about recommended beginner beaches in your area.

- **Pay attention to the water:** Before entering the ocean, observe the waves and study their behavior. Observe how and where the waves break. Keep your eyes on other surfers to learn from their technique and behavior in the water. Paying attention to the water is important for all surfers, both beginners and experienced, as it will allow you to better understand the conditions and make safer decisions.

45

Tips for beginners in the water while surfing:

- **Start small:** It's important to begin with smaller and easier waves. As you gain skills and confidence, you can gradually tackle bigger waves. Follow your instructor's instructions or wait until you're told that you're ready to challenge larger waves.

- **Don't get in the way of experienced surfers:** As a beginner, it's normal to make mistakes and have a lower skill level compared to more experienced surfers. Avoid getting in the way of advanced surfers to prevent causing issues or jeopardizing your safety.

- **Work on your paddling:** Paddling is a fundamental part of surfing. Practice your paddling technique to efficiently move on the board and reach the waves. Maintain a steady rhythm and work on your physical endurance to avoid getting fatigued quickly in the water.

- **Stay perpendicular to the whitewater:** When facing a breaking wave, it's important to maintain a perpendicular position to the whitewater, which is the part of the wave that is breaking. If you're in the wrong position, the wave can drag you down and towards the shore. Learn to read the waves and adjust your position accordingly.

- **Listen to your body:** Pay attention to your body's signals while surfing. If you feel tired, bored, or simply not enjoying the session, it's important to stop and rest. Don't push yourself to continue if you're not in the best physical or mental condition. Surfing should be fun and safe, so respect your limits and come back another day with renewed energy.

46

Introducing children to surfing is an exciting and fun experience.

Here's some information on how to do it:

- **Consider the child's age:** It's important to take the child's age into account when introducing them to surfing. Motor skills and learning ability vary with age, so it's important to adapt lessons and activities accordingly.

- **Water familiarization:** Before introducing the child to surfing, it's crucial for them to feel comfortable in the water. Encourage play and free movement in the water to help the child become familiar with the aquatic environment. Learning to swim and having water confidence are fundamental skills.

- **Learning through play:** Children learn best when they're having fun. Use games and playful activities to teach them basic surfing skills such as balance, coordination, and body control. This will help make surfing an enjoyable and exciting activity for them.

- **Gradual introduction:** As the child grows and develops motor skills, surfing techniques can be gradually introduced. Start with simple activities at the shoreline, such as jumping over small waves or riding bodyboards. As they gain confidence and skills, you can progress to surfing on larger waves with an age-appropriate surfboard.

- **Respect the child's preferences:** It's important not to force a child to surf if they're not comfortable or not showing interest. If the child isn't ready or doesn't want to participate, respect their decision and don't pressure them. Surfing should be a positive and enjoyable experience, and forcing a child can create fear or aversion towards the sport. Encourage the child but allow them to go at their own pace and decide when they're ready to give it a try.

Remember that safety is paramount when teaching children to surf.

Ensure that the child wears appropriate protective gear such as a wetsuit and a leash for the board.

Always supervise the child in the water and teach them about surf safety rules and behavior.

Surfing can be a wonderful activity for children, fostering their confidence, physical skills, and connection with nature.

Enjoy the experience and encourage them to have fun while learning to surf.

47

George Freeth.

Known as the "Father of Modern Surfing," he played a crucial role in introducing surfing to California in the early 20th century.

Born on November 8, 1883, in Honolulu, Hawaii, Freeth was a Hawaiian-Irish professional swimmer and lifeguard.

In 1907, Henry Huntington, a railroad magnate and entrepreneur, hired Freeth to perform surf demonstrations at the Redondo Beach Hotel in California.

Freeth showcased his surfing skills using a traditional Hawaiian wooden board, impressing the audience with his dexterity and style.

Freeth's demonstrations in California marked a milestone in the history of surfing, as it was the first time this sport was witnessed on the West Coast of the United States.

His performance generated great interest and enthusiasm among spectators, and surfing began to gain popularity in the region.

In addition to his demonstrations, Freeth also played a significant role as a surfing instructor.

He taught many Californians how to surf, imparting his knowledge and passion for the sport.

His teaching style influenced the way surfing was practiced in California, laying the groundwork for the development of modern surfing in the area.

George Freeth was a surfing pioneer, and his legacy endures in the surf culture of California and beyond.

His contribution to the sport has been recognized, and his name has become synonymous with the early days of surfing on the West Coast of the United States.

Today, California is globally known for its excellent surfing conditions and attracts surfers from around the world.

Surfing has become a global phenomenon, but its introduction in California and its subsequent expansion would not have been possible without the influence of George Freeth and his pivotal role in the birth of modern surfing.

48

Surfing is a diverse and exciting sport that offers different styles to suit the preferences and abilities of surfers.

- **Shortboard:** It is the most popular and widely practiced surfing style. The short surfboards used in this style are generally smaller, thinner, and lighter, making them highly maneuverable on waves. The shortboard allows for quick turns, radical maneuvers, and aerial tricks, being the preferred style for many professional surfers.

- **Longboard:** It is a more relaxed and classic surfing style. The surfboards used in longboarding are longer and wider, providing greater stability and ease of catching waves. Longboarders often focus on smooth and elegant gliding, performing gentle turns and flowing with the wave. This style evokes nostalgia for the early days of surfing and is considered an art form in itself.

- **Fish:** It is a surfing style that utilizes shorter and wider boards with a distinctive "fish" shape. These boards are fast and agile, designed to easily catch small to medium-sized waves. The fish style is known for its ability to generate speed and perform quick maneuvers in smoother conditions.

- **Gun:** It is a type of surfboard specially designed to tackle large and powerful waves. These boards are longer and narrower, allowing them to glide at high speeds on big waves. Surfers who practice the gun style often seek the challenge of riding big waves and performing vertical and fast maneuvers in extreme conditions.

- **Hybrid:** As the name suggests, hybrid boards combine characteristics from different surfing styles. These boards aim to find a balance between the maneuverability of a shortboard and the stability of a longboard, providing surfers with versatility to adapt to a wide range of wave conditions.

It's worth noting that there are many other styles and variations within the world of surfing, and surfers often develop their own customized style.

The choice of surfing style depends on individual preferences, the surfer's skill level, and the sea conditions.

Exploring different surfing styles can be exciting and allow surfers to experience different sensations and challenges in the water.

49

The art of shortboarding.

It focuses on the skill and mastery of the smaller and more maneuverable surfboard, known as a shortboard.

Key information about shortboarding:

- **Board size and shape:** Short surfboards are typically around 5 to 7 feet (1.5 to 2.1 meters) in length and are narrower and thinner compared to longer surfboards. This shape allows for greater maneuverability and responsiveness on waves.

- **Paddling technique:** Paddling is a crucial aspect of shortboarding. Since the boards are smaller, they require more effort to paddle through waves and reach the breaking point. Developing an efficient paddling technique is important to maintain speed and stability in the water.

- **Takeoff:** The takeoff in shortboarding is a critical moment. It requires a good sense of anticipation and timing to paddle into the wave, quickly pop up, and stand up on the board at the right moment. Practice and experience will help perfect this skill.

- **Maneuvers and turns:** Shortboarding offers the opportunity to perform a variety of dynamic maneuvers and turns on the wave. By mastering the use of the board's edges, surfers can execute quick, vertical, and radical turns. Some common maneuvers include the cutback (turn at the top of the wave), floater (riding above a closing section), and reentry (sharp turn after a previous maneuver).

- **Timing mastery:** Surfers must learn to read waves and anticipate the right moment to perform maneuvers and make decisions on the wave. This includes choosing the best line to ride the wave, executing turns at the optimal point, and exiting the wave at the right time.

- **Developing personal style:** As surfers gain experience in shortboarding, they can develop their own personalized style. This involves combining moves, fluidity, and individual expression on the waves. Personal style is what sets each surfer apart and adds an artistic dimension to shortboarding.

50

The Bachelor's Degree in Surfing at the University of Plymouth is a pioneering academic program that focuses on the study of surfing from multiple perspectives.

Relevant information about this program:

-Program nature: The Bachelor's Degree in Surfing is a full-time undergraduate course offered by the University of Plymouth, located in the United Kingdom. It is a multidisciplinary program that combines theoretical and practical aspects related to surfing.

-Program content: The curriculum covers a wide range of topics, including surfing history and culture, oceanography, meteorology, biomechanics, health and fitness, sustainability and environmental management in surfing, sports psychology, marketing and entrepreneurship in the surf industry, among others.

-Practical focus: While the program has a significant academic component, it also emphasizes the practical application of acquired knowledge. Students have the opportunity to participate in surf sessions, develop technical skills, learn about water safety, and conduct practical research related to surfing.

-Equipment and resources: The University of Plymouth has specialized facilities and equipment for the study of surfing, including surfboards, wetsuits, surf simulators, and access to nearby beaches. This allows students to experience and develop skills in a real-world environment.

-Careers and opportunities: The Bachelor's Degree in Surfing prepares students for a variety of careers in the surf industry. They can choose to work as surf instructors, coaches, surf scientists, surf center managers, marketing and branding experts, or even start their own surf-related business. Additionally, the degree can also provide a solid foundation for further postgraduate studies in related areas.

-Importance of sustainable surfing: The program emphasizes the importance of sustainability and environmental responsibility in surfing. Students will learn about sustainable practices in the surf industry and how to minimize negative impacts on coastal and oceanic ecosystems.

-Recognition and prestige: The Bachelor's Degree in Surfing from the University of Plymouth has gained national and international recognition as an innovative initiative in surf education. The university has established partnerships and collaborations with organizations and professionals in the surf industry to enrich the educational experience of students.

51

Ride Barrels.

Also known as surfing tubes or pipelines, it is considered one of the most exciting and challenging moments in surfing.

Information about this unique experience:

- **What is a barrel?** In surfing, a barrel refers to the formation of a hollow and cylindrical wave that breaks over itself, creating a perfect tube. The surfer can enter this tube and ride inside it as the wave moves towards the shore.

- **The thrill of riding barrels:** Surfing inside the tube provides a sense of adrenaline and intense excitement. The surfer finds themselves in a confined and narrow space, with the wave breaking above their head and behind them, creating an almost surreal environment.

- **Skill and experience required:** Riding barrels is considered an advanced skill in surfing. It requires great technique, knowledge of the wave's breaking point, and reading the ocean to choose the right wave. Additionally, the ability to maintain balance and proper posture while inside the barrel is essential.

- **Associated dangers:** Although riding barrels can be thrilling, it also carries significant risks. The surfer is exposed to the forces of nature and may face dangerous situations, such as getting caught inside the barrel if the wave collapses prematurely. Additionally, the pressure and force of the water can be intense, leading to falls or injuries.

- **Iconic locations:** Some beaches and surf breaks worldwide are famous for offering favorable conditions for riding barrels. Destinations like Pipeline in Hawaii, Teahupoo in Tahiti, Supertubos in Portugal, and Mundaka in Spain are known for their perfect and challenging tubes.

- **Surf culture and barrels:** Riding barrels is an important aspect of surf culture and is considered a notable achievement for many surfers. The most impressive and longest tubes are admired and respected in the surfing community.

52

The survey conducted by American Surf Magazine, which found that 66% of surfers think about sharks while in the water, reflects the common concern some surfers may have regarding the presence of these animals in the ocean.

However, it is important to note that this concern may vary among surfers and depend on factors such as geographic location and personal experiences.

It is true that the presence of sharks in the ocean is a reality, and surfers are aware of it.

The expression "men in gray suits" is used in the Anglo-Saxon surfing world to refer to sharks, alluding to the gray color of their skin.

This expression is a colloquial and humorous way of referring to these animals.

It is important to highlight that while sharks may be present in surf areas, actual encounters between sharks and surfers are extremely rare.

Shark attacks are infrequent events, and the chances of being attacked by a shark while surfing are extremely low.

Nevertheless, it is understandable that the idea of sharks may generate some apprehension in certain surfers.

To alleviate this concern, it is recommended to follow established safety precautions, such as avoiding surfing in areas with known shark concentrations, staying informed about local conditions, and following guidelines for safe behavior in the water.

It is important to remember that surfing is an exciting and rewarding sport, and the majority of surfers continue to enjoy the waves without the presence of sharks hindering their full experience in the water.

53

The claim that the first written account of surfing was given in 1778 by Captain James Cook when he visited Hawaii is a widely accepted historical fact.

James Cook, a famous British explorer, arrived at the Hawaiian islands during his third voyage to the Pacific.

During his stay, Cook and his crew observed the native Hawaiians practicing surfing on the waves.

In his account, Cook described the activity of surfing in the following words: "I could not help concluding that this man felt the most supreme pleasure while he was driven so fast and so smoothly by the sea."

His observations and written records helped introduce surfing to Western consciousness and were one of the earliest documented accounts of this activity.

It is important to note that surfing had been an integral part of Hawaiian culture for centuries before Cook's arrival.

Native Hawaiians had been surfing long before Cook and Western explorers reached the islands.

However, Cook's account provided one of the first written records of Hawaiian surfing and helped spread its popularity in the Western world.

54

The term "hodad" is used in surf culture to refer to a person who presents themselves as a surfer but lacks real surfing skills or a genuine commitment to the sport.

It refers to someone who pretends to be a surfer but lacks the experience and knowledge necessary to engage in surfing authentically.

The term "hodad" originated in the 1960s in California, United States, during the height of surf and beach culture.

It was used to describe individuals who dressed in the typical appearance of surfers, such as beachwear, surf shirts, and sandals, but lacked the actual ability to surf or a true interest in the sport.

"Hodads" are often associated with behaviors that go against authenticity and respect within surf culture.

They can be seen as impostors or intruders attempting to appropriate the image and attitude of real surfers without having a genuine commitment to the sport.

It is important to mention that the term "hodad" can have different connotations depending on the region and context in which it is used.

Sometimes, it is used derogatorily to indicate someone pretending to be a surfer but lacking authenticity and necessary knowledge, while other times it may be used more lightly or humorously to refer to someone who is enjoying themselves at the beach without actually practicing surfing.

55

In 2016, surfer Alison Teal accomplished a remarkable feat by surfing near an active volcano.

Alison Teal is known for her extreme adventures and her commitment to exploring unique locations around the world.

The exact location of the volcano where Teal performed this feat is not specified in the question, so specific cases involving Teal and volcanoes at different times and places should be considered.

One notable event in Alison Teal's career is her experience on the Big Island of Hawaii.

In 2016, during a volcanic eruption of the Kilauea volcano, Teal approached the volcano and surfed in the waters near the areas affected by the lava.

The flowing lava into the ocean created a unique and dangerous scene, but Teal ventured to surf in those extreme conditions.

It is important to note that engaging in activities near active volcanoes carries significant safety risks.

Proximity to lava and volcanic gases can be extremely dangerous and potentially fatal.

Surfers and adventurers who venture into such situations should take proper precautions, have experience in the activity, and follow the guidance of experts and local authorities.

Alison Teal's feat of surfing near an active volcano showcases her bravery and passion for pushing new boundaries in the world of surfing.

56

The sea foam that killed 5 surfers.

The tragic incident occurred at Scheveningen beach in the Netherlands due to a phenomenon known as sea foam.

Sea foam is a formation of white foam that occurs when seawater contains high levels of organic matter, such as algae or phytoplankton, and is agitated intensely by waves and currents.

In this specific case, the sea foam reached a height of over one meter, which made rescue efforts challenging.

Weather conditions, including strong winds and high waves, further complicated the situation.

Despite the efforts of the police, firefighters, coast guard, and other authorities, only four out of the five affected surfers were successfully rescued.

The fifth surfer was spotted but unfortunately swallowed by the waters and could not be rescued.

The tragic incident caused shock and grief in the community of The Hague, the city where Scheveningen beach is located.

The mayor of the city, Johan Remkes, described the events as a "terrible tragedy."

Sea foam is a natural phenomenon that can occur in various parts of the world and, under extreme conditions, can pose a danger to surfers and other people in the water.

It is important to be aware of the risks associated with sea conditions and take proper precautions when engaging in water sports.

57

High sea foam.

This specific phenomenon is related to the presence of a type of algae that inhabits the waters of the North Sea.

During spring, these algae undergo a blooming period in which they reproduce massively.

At the end of this period, the algae cells disintegrate, releasing a similar residual material.

Wind and waves play a significant role in the formation of foam.

When the algae disintegrate, the residual material mixes with the water and is agitated by the waves and wind.

This agitation causes the formation of bubbles and the accumulation of foam on the water surface.

In the case of the accident at Scheveningen beach, the presence of strong north winds contributed to an increased level of foam.

The wind pushes and disperses the foam towards the shore, generating significant accumulations along the coastline.

Researchers are studying this phenomenon to better understand the conditions that allow for the formation of such a dense layer of foam.

The University of Vienna has conducted research on this topic, and their findings suggest that the phenomenon can occur in almost any natural body of water, provided the right circumstances are present.

58

The high heels surfing tournament.

Organized by a group of Russian female surfers at Kuta Beach on the island of Bali, it was a unique and unconventional event.

The idea originated from a 28-year-old surfer who was inspired by a student who wanted to combine her passion for dancing and surfing by wearing high heels for photoshoots.

The surfer decided to seize the idea and organize a surfing competition in high heels, challenging participants to surf with heels measuring between 8 and 10 cm in height.

This challenge adds an additional level of difficulty to the sport of surfing, as balancing and maneuvering on a surfboard requires balance and dexterity.

The event took place at Kuta Beach, known for its waves and surfer atmosphere.

Participants faced the challenge of surfing in high heels, providing an unusual and eye-catching spectacle for the audience.

The tournament combined a passion for surfing with fashion and style, creating a unique experience for participants and spectators.

Although surfing in high heels may seem fun and extravagant, it is important to note that it involves additional risks.

Balance and stability can be compromised when wearing heels, increasing the chances of falls and injuries.

Participants should take extra precautions and be aware of the potential risks associated with this challenge.

59

Surfboard tails are a crucial part of their design and have a significant impact on the performance and maneuverability of the board in the water.

There are four common types of tails and their importance:

- **Squash Tail:** It is one of the most popular and versatile shapes. It has a square or slightly rounded appearance at the back of the board. This tail provides a good balance between grip and release, making it suitable for a wide variety of wave conditions. It is stable and facilitates quick transitions between turns.

- **Pin Tail:** It has a narrower and pointed shape, similar to a pin or a cone. This tail is suitable for surfing in big and powerful waves as it provides excellent control and grip in more challenging conditions. The pointed shape helps the board maintain its line in fast waves and allows for more pronounced turns.

- **Round Tail:** It has a smooth and curved shape at the back of the board. This tail offers a good balance between grip and maneuverability. It is especially effective in smaller and slower waves, allowing for quick and fluid turns. The round tail also helps maintain stability in more turbulent conditions.

- **Swallow Tail:** Also known as a swallowtail, it has a distinctive double notch shape at the back of the board. This tail enhances maneuverability and grip in faster and curvier wave conditions. The tail shape helps release water and provides a smooth transition between turns.

Choosing the right tail will depend on factors such as the type of waves that will be surfed most often, the surfer's skill level, and personal preferences.

Experienced surfers often have multiple boards with different tail shapes to accommodate different conditions.

It is important to try out different tail types to find the one that best suits your surfing style and the waves you typically encounter.

60

The most iconic surfboards.

- **Duke Kahanamoku's Solid Wood Board:** Duke Kahanamoku, known as the father of modern surfing, popularized surfing in the 1910s. His handcrafted solid wood board has become a symbol of the early days of modern surfing and has inspired generations of surfers.

- **Malibu Chip:** Developed in the 1940s by Matt Kivlin, this hollow wooden board was one of the first to introduce stabilization through fins. The design of the Malibu Chip laid the foundation for future surfboards, and its popularity contributed to the growth of surfing in California.

- **Hobie Alter's Foam Board:** In the 1950s, Hobie Alter revolutionized the surfing industry by introducing polyurethane foam boards. These boards were lighter, more durable, and easier to manufacture compared to traditional wooden boards. The development of foam boards allowed for greater access to surfing and opened the doors for the sport's massive growth.

- **Lightning Bolt:** Lightning Bolt boards, designed by Gerry Lopez and Jack Shipley in the 1970s, became a symbol of high-performance surfing and style. These boards, known for their distinctive lightning bolt logo, were used by many prominent surfers of the time and helped establish the brand as one of the most recognized in the industry.

- **Fish Board:** Created by Steve Lis in the 1970s, it revolutionized surfboard design. Characterized by its short, wide shape and swallowtail, the Fish Board provided increased speed and maneuverability in smaller waves. This innovation influenced the development of other board shapes and experimentation with alternative designs.

- **Thruster:** Developed by Simon Anderson in 1980, it introduced the three-fin system that became the industry standard. This design provided greater control and maneuverability in waves, allowing surfers to perform quick and radical turns. The Thruster had a significant impact on the evolution of high-performance surfing.

These are just some of the most iconic surfboards of all time, but there are many others that have made their mark in the history of surfing.

Each board represents an important stage in the sport's evolution and has influenced how it is practiced and enjoyed today.

61

Customizing a surfboard.

It is a way to personalize and tailor your equipment to your preferences and surfing style.

Some aspects to consider:

- **Graphic design:** You can add unique designs, logos, or patterns to your board using paint or decals. This will give it a customized and distinctive look.

- **Colors and finishes:** You can choose the colors of the resin used on the board as well as the final finish. Some surfers opt for glossy, matte, or even gradient effects.

- **Fins:** Fins are an essential part of a surfboard and they affect its performance. You can customize the type of fins you use, such as classic single fin, twin fins, thruster (three fins), or quad (four fins). Additionally, you can choose different materials and sizes of fins to adjust the speed, stability, and grip of your board.

- **Tail pad:** It is an adhesive pad placed on the rear of the board to provide traction and grip to the surfer's back foot. You can customize the design, color, and placement of the tail pad according to your preferences.

- **Deck grip:** In addition to the tail pad, you can add a grip pad on the top of the board, known as deck grip. This will provide better grip and stability to your feet during surfing. There are different designs and materials available to choose from.

- **Reinforcements and repairs:** If you have a surfboard that needs repairs or reinforcements, you can customize the type of reinforcement used or choose patches of different colors to add a personalized touch to the repaired areas.

It is important to remember that when customizing your surfboard, you should consider the characteristics and technical specifications that suit your surfing style and skill level.

Consulting with a shaper or surfboard expert can be helpful in achieving the best results.

Also, keep in mind that some changes in the board's design and setup can affect its performance, so it is recommended to test the adjustments before making permanent changes.

62

Tips for tuning your surfboard:

- **Regular cleaning:** Keep your surfboard clean and free from dirt, sand, and salt deposits. Rinse it with fresh water after each session and occasionally use a mild cleanser to remove stubborn stains.

- **Damage inspection:** Regularly inspect your board for possible damage such as dings, cracks, or resin delamination. Repair any damage promptly to prevent it from worsening and affecting the board's performance.

- **Proper waxing:** Apply a layer of surf wax on the top of the board to provide traction and prevent slipping. Make sure to apply the wax evenly and according to the water and temperature conditions.

- **Fin adjustment:** Experiment with different fin setups to find the best one for your surfing style and the ocean conditions. You can adjust the position and angle of the fins to achieve more grip, speed, or maneuverability.

- **Fin replacement:** If your fins are worn out or damaged, consider replacing them. Worn-out fins can affect the board's performance, so keep an eye on their condition and change them when necessary.

- **Ding repair:** Dings are common in surfboards and can affect their performance. Use a repair resin and a ding repair kit to fix the damages. Follow the instructions in the kit or consult a professional if you're unsure how to do it correctly.

- **Grip adjustment:** If you use a grip pad on the top of the board, make sure it is properly adhered and in the right position. Replace the grip if it is worn out or doesn't provide sufficient traction.

- **Proper storage:** When you're not using your board, store it in a safe place protected from direct sunlight, excessive moisture, and abrupt temperature changes. Use a surfboard cover to protect it during transportation and storage.

63

Most common mistakes when choosing a new surfboard:

- **Choosing a board based solely on its appearance:** While it's understandable that you want a board that looks good, you shouldn't make your decision solely based on its looks. Make sure to consider other key factors such as your skill level, weight, height, and the type of waves you plan to surf.

- **Buying an overly advanced board:** If you're a beginner or have limited surfing skills, avoid boards designed for advanced surfers. These boards are often thinner, narrower, and less stable, making them difficult to handle for beginners.

- **Not considering your skill level:** It's important to choose a board that suits your skill level. If you're a beginner, opt for a larger, more stable, and easy-to-handle board. As your skill improves, you can transition to smaller and higher-performance boards.

- **Not consulting with an expert:** If you're unsure about which board to choose, it's advisable to seek guidance from a surfing expert such as a shaper or experienced surfer. They can assess your needs and help you find the right board for you.

- **Not considering wave conditions:** The type of waves you plan to surf in also influences your board choice. If you'll mainly be surfing small and mellow waves, a board with more volume and flotation will be more suitable. If you plan to surf big and powerful waves, you can opt for a smaller and more maneuverable board.

- **Not testing the board before buying:** It's always recommended to test a board before making a purchase, if possible. By surfing with it, you'll have a better idea of how it feels under your feet and if it suits your surfing style.

- **Not considering your weight and height:** Your weight and height are important factors to consider when choosing a surfboard. These factors will determine the appropriate volume and length of the board for you to have good balance and flotation in the water.

64

Some of the best beaches for surfing:

- **Pipeline, Oahu, Hawaii:** Considered one of the most challenging and iconic waves in the world, Pipeline attracts expert surfers from around the globe. Its hollow and powerful waves make this spot a true challenge.

- **Supertubes, Jeffreys Bay, South Africa:** Jeffreys Bay is famous for its long and fast waves in the area known as Supertubes. It's an iconic surf destination and hosts high-level competition events.

- **Teahupoo, Tahiti:** Known for its massive and dangerous waves, Teahupoo is an extreme surf spot that attracts the most fearless surfers. Its hollow and powerful breakers are quite a challenge.

- **Uluwatu, Bali, Indonesia:** Bali is renowned for its incredible surf beaches, and Uluwatu is one of the standout spots. With consistent and tubular waves, it's a favorite destination for surfers from around the world.

- **Banzai Pipeline, Oahu, Hawaii:** Another iconic spot in Hawaii, Banzai Pipeline is known for its big and tubular waves that can be dangerous. It attracts professional surfers looking to tackle its challenging breakers.

- **Gold Coast, Queensland, Australia:** The Gold Coast of Australia is famous for its numerous world-class surf breaks. From Snapper Rocks to Kirra, there are waves for surfers of all levels and preferences.

- **Hossegor, France:** Hossegor is known as the surfing mecca in Europe. Its consistent and powerful waves attract surfers from all over the continent, especially during the famous annual Quiksilver Pro France event.

These are just some of the many beaches worldwide that offer excellent surfing conditions.

Each location has its own personality and unique features, so exploring and discovering new spots is part of the excitement of surfing.

65

Some of the worst beaches for surfing.

These can be considered "worst" for surfing due to various factors such as lack of consistent waves, rocky or sandy bottoms, wind direction, or the presence of dangerous currents.

- **Copacabana Beach, Rio de Janeiro, Brazil:** Although it is a very popular and beautiful beach, the waves at Copacabana are generally small and inconsistent for surfing. Additionally, strong currents and the large number of people in the water can make surfing challenging and potentially dangerous.

- **Marina Beach, Chennai, India:** While Marina Beach is one of the longest beaches in the world, it is not known for having good waves for surfing. The sea conditions are generally calm and do not offer the necessary characteristics for satisfying surfing.

- **Blackpool, England:** Although Blackpool is a popular tourist beach, the conditions for surfing are mostly poor. The waves are usually small and inconsistent, and the presence of piers and coastal structures can further hinder surfing.

- **Eastern Mediterranean:** Although the Mediterranean Sea has beautiful beaches, the conditions for surfing are generally not optimal in the eastern part of the Mediterranean. The lack of winds and absence of large wave systems make it difficult to find suitable waves for surfing in this region.

It is important to note that surfing conditions can change, and even in these beaches considered "worst," there may be specific moments or conditions when it is possible to surf.

66

The most expensive surfboard in the world.

It is known as "The Rampant," created by Australian shaper Roy Stuart.

It was auctioned in 2014 for the incredible sum of $1.3 million to an anonymous collector.

This surfboard is considered a unique work of art and is highly valued for its exclusivity and meticulous design.

"The Rampant" is handcrafted with high-quality materials and luxurious details.

The board has a polyurethane foam core and is coated with a layer of fiberglass to provide strength and durability.

Additionally, it is adorned with 23-carat gold accents, including the brand logo and ornamental patterns on the underside of the board.

The value of this surfboard is attributed to its exclusivity, custom design, and the reputation of shaper Roy Stuart.

Furthermore, the fact that it was auctioned for such a high amount makes it the most expensive surfboard recorded to date.

It is important to note that while "The Rampant" is the most expensive known surfboard, there are other custom and limited edition boards that can also have a considerably high price.

The value of a surfboard can vary based on various factors, such as the shaper, materials used, design, exclusivity, and market demand.

67

Shark attacks on surfers.

They are uncommon events, but throughout history, there have been some documented incidents.

- **Shark Attack in New Jersey (1916):** This was one of the most famous cases of shark attacks on surfers. Along the coast of New Jersey, a series of shark attacks were recorded in July 1916, including the infamous incident in Matawan Creek where a shark attacked multiple people, resulting in the death of four individuals. This event inspired Steven Spielberg's novel and film "Jaws."

- **Shark Attack in Western Australia (2011-2013):** Between 2011 and 2013, a series of shark attacks were recorded in the Western Australia region. Several surfers were attacked, some of them fatally. These incidents led to the implementation of shark prevention and control measures in the area, such as the installation of nets and the implementation of observation programs.

- **Shark Attack in Hawaii (2015):** In April 2015, a surfer was attacked by a shark at Oahu's beach in Hawaii. The surfer suffered leg injuries but managed to reach the shore and receive medical attention. This incident raised concerns within the Hawaiian surfing community, leading to enhanced safety measures on the beaches.

- **Shark Attack in South Africa (2015):** In June 2015, a surfer was attacked by a great white shark at Nahoon Reef Beach near East London, South Africa. Fortunately, the surfer managed to escape with minor injuries after fighting off the shark and receiving assistance from other surfers.

- **Shark Attack in California, United States (2020):** In May 2020, a surfer was attacked by a great white shark at Santa Cruz Beach, California. The surfer sustained serious leg injuries but was able to reach the shore and be rescued by other surfers and lifeguards.

It is important to note that shark attacks are rare events, and the likelihood of encountering a shark while surfing is very low.

68

There are some measures that surfers can take to reduce the risk of shark attacks while surfing.

- **Stay informed:** It is important to be aware of local reports on shark sightings or areas with recent shark attacks. Follow the recommendations of local authorities and stay updated on sea conditions.

- **Avoid areas known for shark presence:** Research beaches and surf spots known for high shark activity and avoid them if possible. Pay attention to lifeguard warnings and advice from locals.

- **Don't surf alone:** Always try to surf with other surfers. Besides being safer, the presence of others in the water can help deter sharks.

- **Avoid areas with seal or sea lion presence:** These animals are natural prey for sharks, and their presence can attract them. If you see a colony of seals or sea lions near the surf zone, it is advisable to find another place to surf.

- **Avoid surfing near river mouths or areas with turbid waters:** These areas can be natural habitats for sharks and often have limited visibility, making it difficult to spot potentially dangerous sharks.

- **Avoid surfing in low visibility conditions or dark waters:** If the water is murky or there is low visibility due to the time of day, weather conditions, or presence of algae, it's best not to surf. Limited visibility increases the risk of surprise encounters with sharks.

- **Avoid wearing bright jewelry or flashy-colored clothing:** The reflections from bright jewelry or vivid colors can attract the attention of sharks. It's better to opt for more discreet colors and patterns while in the water.

- **Respect sharks:** If you encounter a shark while surfing, stay calm and slowly move away from the area. Do not attempt to interact with or scare the shark, as this can provoke an aggressive response.

69

There are several products and devices on the market that are used as deterrent measures to keep sharks away from surfers.

- **Acoustic devices:** Some devices emit low-frequency sounds believed to deter sharks. These devices use sonic pulses or acoustic signals to interfere with the sharks' detection and orientation.

- **Electronic devices:** There are electronic devices that generate electric or magnetic fields around the surfer. It is supposed that these fields can interfere with the sharks' electric sensors and discourage them from approaching.

- **Visual devices:** Some products use visual patterns or LED lights to disorient sharks and prevent them from approaching. These patterns can be seen as a danger signal by sharks, making them stay away.

- **Scent devices:** Some surfers use chemicals that emit strong and unpleasant odors for sharks. It is believed that these odors can repel sharks and prevent them from approaching.

- **Neoprene suits with camouflage patterns:** Some surfers wear neoprene suits with camouflage patterns designed to confuse the surfer's silhouette and make them less visible to sharks.

It's important to note that the effectiveness of these products and devices may vary, and there is no foolproof solution to avoid shark encounters.

70

Mass brawls among surfers, also known as "surf brawls" or "surf fights," are uncommon incidents but have occurred on some occasions.

These fights can arise for various reasons, such as competition for waves, personal disagreements, territorial issues, or differences in skill level and water etiquette.

When a mass brawl among surfers occurs, it usually involves multiple participants and can take place both in and out of the water.

These fights tend to be chaotic and may involve punches, shoving, heated arguments, and even the use of blunt objects.

It's important to highlight that this kind of behavior is not representative of the majority of surfers who seek to enjoy the sport in a camaraderie and respectful environment.

Mass brawls are considered inappropriate and dangerous behavior and can result in injuries for those involved.

To avoid these situations, it's essential to follow certain water etiquette guidelines and maintain a respectful attitude towards other surfers.

Some recommendations include:

- Respect the rotation: Waiting for your turn and not trying to catch every wave can help avoid conflicts with other surfers.

- Clear communication: Using clear signals or words to communicate with other surfers and avoid misunderstandings.

- Keep calm: Control emotions and avoid reacting aggressively to conflict situations.

- Respect local rules: Know and follow the rules and norms of the beach or spot where you're surfing.

- Be safety-conscious: Prioritize your own safety and that of others by avoiding dangerous or irresponsible maneuvers.

In case of witnessing or being involved in a mass brawl, it's important to seek the assistance of local authorities, such as lifeguards or the police, and cooperate to resolve the conflict in the most peaceful way possible.

71

The number of fins to be placed on a surfboard can vary depending on several factors, such as the type of wave, surfing style, and the surfer's personal preferences.

- Single Fin: This is the most classic design, consisting of a single central fin. This type of configuration provides stability and good directional control. Single fin boards are popular in retro and classic-style surfboards.

- Twin Fin: It consists of two fins, usually placed near the board's side edges. Twin fin boards offer a loose and agile feel, ideal for performing quick and fluid maneuvers.

- Thruster: This is the most common configuration in modern surfboards. It consists of three fins: a central fin and two smaller side fins. This configuration offers a good balance of stability, control, and maneuverability. It is suitable for a wide variety of surf conditions and surfing styles.

- Quad: It consists of four fins, usually two fins in the front and two fins in the back of the board. This configuration provides excellent speed and grip in faster and hollower waves. It is especially popular among surfers looking to perform radical maneuvers and make the most of challenging surf conditions.

- 5-fin setup: Some boards are designed to be compatible with different fin configurations, allowing the surfer to choose between a thruster (3 fins) or quad (4 fins) setup depending on the surf conditions. This option provides versatility and the ability to adapt to different types of waves.

72

Surfing made its debut as an Olympic sport at the Tokyo 2020 Olympic Games, which took place in the summer of 2021 due to the delay caused by the COVID-19 pandemic.

It was included as an official discipline and took place at Tsurigasaki Beach, located in Chiba Prefecture, Japan.

Surfing was added to the Olympic program as part of the International Olympic Committee's (IOC) efforts to attract a younger audience and diversify the sports represented in the Olympic Games.

This inclusion was significant news for the surfing community as it granted officially recognized Olympic sport status.

The surfing competition at the Tokyo 2020 Olympic Games featured the participation of 40 surfers, 20 men and 20 women, from different countries around the world.

Surfers competed in various rounds, including qualifying rounds, elimination rounds, and the finals.

The format of Olympic surfing competition consisted of a series of heats (rounds) in which surfers had a designated time to catch waves and showcase their skills.

Judges evaluated performances based on the difficulty of maneuvers executed, speed, power, and flow of the surfers.

Surfing is a sport that combines balance, strength, and skill in the water.

Surfers aim to ride waves with their surfboards and perform maneuvers such as turns, tubes, and jumps to achieve the highest possible score.

The quality and size of the waves can influence the surfers' performance, making ocean conditions an important factor in the competition.

Olympic surfing has generated significant interest worldwide, providing a global platform for the best surfers to showcase their talent and compete for Olympic medals.

It has also increased the visibility and recognition of the sport, potentially having a positive impact on its development and popularity internationally.

It's important to note that surfing is not only an Olympic sport but also a recreational activity and a way of life for many people worldwide.

In addition to its involvement in the Olympic Games, there are professional surfing competitions and circuits, such as the World Surf League (WSL) Championship Tour, which attract surfers and fans from around the globe.

73

**In 1975, Australian surfer Tony Alva made history by
installing the first camera on a surfboard.**

He was a true pioneer in the use of cameras in surfing, which would eventually
become a common practice in the surfing community.

The idea of placing a camera on a surfboard allowed surfers to capture unique
images and perspectives of their maneuvers and the waves they were surfing.

This opened up a new world of possibilities in terms of documenting and
visualizing the surfing experience from the surfer's own perspective.

The first camera used by Tony Alva was a 16mm film camera, housed in a
waterproof casing and attached to the front of his surfboard.

The camera was protected to prevent water damage and impacts during surfing.

The use of cameras in surfing has evolved significantly since Tony Alva's early
days.

Nowadays, compact and waterproof action cameras, such as the popular GoPro,
are primarily used, and they can be mounted on the front, back, or sides of the
surfboard.

These cameras allow surfers to capture high-quality images and record high-
definition videos of their surf sessions.

They are also capable of capturing slow-motion footage, time-lapses, and live
streaming through applications and online platforms.

The use of cameras in surfing has had a significant impact on the surfing
community, as it has provided a way to document and share experiences in the
water.

Surfers can review and analyze their waves, share their best moments with friends
and followers on social media, and also use the images and videos to improve their
surfing technique and style.

Furthermore, cameras on surfboards have also allowed the capture of stunning
and cinematic images of surfers in action, contributing to the promotion and
dissemination of the sport worldwide through films, documentaries, and online
content.

74

Eco-friendly surfboards.

In response to the growing awareness of sustainability, a variety of eco-friendly surfboards have been developed to reduce the environmental impact associated with the manufacturing and use of traditional boards made from polyurethane foam and polyester resin.

These eco-friendly boards are made with renewable, recycled, or more sustainable materials such as cork, bamboo, and natural fibers.

-Cork: Cork is a natural and renewable material that has been used in the manufacturing of surfboards. Cork boards typically have a cork core with a fiberglass and eco-resin covering. Cork is lightweight, buoyant, and has cushioning properties, making it ideal for surfboard construction.

-Bamboo: Bamboo has become a popular material for the production of eco-friendly surfboards. Bamboo is a fast-growing and renewable plant that can replace polyurethane foam in the board's core. Bamboo fibers are laminated with eco-resins and fiberglass to create a durable and lightweight board.

-Recycled Wood: Some eco-friendly surfboards are made using recycled wood, such as reclaimed pallet or construction woods. These boards are constructed in layers, using laminating and pressing techniques to achieve the proper shape and structure.

-Natural Fibers: Instead of conventional fiberglass, some eco-friendly surfboards utilize natural fibers such as linen or hemp in the deck and reinforcement construction. These fibers are more sustainable compared to synthetic fibers and offer similar performance.

-Recycled Materials: Another option is to use recycled materials in surfboard manufacturing. This can include recycled foams like recycled expanded polystyrene (EPS) and resins made from renewable or recycled materials. By recycling materials, the demand for new resources is reduced, and waste is avoided.

It is important to note that eco-friendly surfboards may have slightly different characteristics and performance compared to traditional boards, as the materials and manufacturing methods can influence their flexibility, durability, and feel in the water.

However, many people find that these boards offer a satisfying balance between performance and environmental sustainability.

75

Night surfing.

It is an exciting and unique practice in which surfers take advantage of the nighttime hours to surf the waves with surfboards equipped with built-in LED lights.

This activity has gained popularity in recent years and has allowed surfers to experience a new dimension in their passion for surfing.

Surfboards with built-in LED lights generally feature light strips or LED disks strategically placed on the bottom or edges of the board.

These lights are waterproof and designed to be durable and safe during surfing.

The use of LED lights on night surfboards not only adds an impressive visual component but also offers several practical benefits.

LED lights can help surfers have better visibility of the waves and water conditions, which can be especially useful on dark nights or with low lighting.

Additionally, the lights can also help surfers be more visible to other surfers in the water, enhancing safety.

It is important to note that night surfing may require additional precautions due to reduced visibility.

Surfers practicing this activity should be aware of their abilities and limitations and take appropriate safety measures, such as surfing in known areas and in groups, using proper protective equipment, and following local regulations and sea conditions.

Night surfing can provide a unique and magical experience for surfers, allowing them to enjoy the waves and the beauty of the ocean under moonlight and LED lights.

Furthermore, the calm and serene atmosphere of the night can provide a sense of tranquility and connection with nature.

76

Cold water surfing.

It is a challenging and exciting practice in which surfers venture to surf in places where water temperatures are extremely cold, such as Norway, Canada, and Alaska.

Despite the low temperatures and the presence of ice blocks, these brave surfers find a way to enjoy the waves in unique and spectacular environments.

Important aspects to consider:

-Special wetsuits: To face the cold water temperatures, surfers use wetsuits specifically designed for cold water conditions. These suits are usually thicker and provide greater thermal insulation than conventional wetsuits. They can range from 5 to 7 mm in thickness in the body, with longer sleeves and legs to provide more protection.

-Additional accessories: In addition to wetsuits, surfers in cold water may use additional accessories to stay warm, such as gloves, booties, and neoprene hoods. These accessories help protect the extremities from the cold and retain body heat.

-Safety precautions: Surfing in cold water presents unique challenges in terms of safety. Surfers must be aware of potential dangers such as hypothermia and floating ice blocks. It is important to be prepared and take additional precautions, such as surfing in groups, informing someone about the plans, being knowledgeable about currents, and having an emergency plan in case of any eventuality.

-Water and ice conditions: Cold water surfing involves dealing with the presence of ice blocks in the water, which can be an additional challenge for surfers. It is important to carefully assess water and ice conditions before venturing out. Some surfers prefer to surf in breaks where ice is less present, while others may seek areas where ice blocks form unique and challenging waves.

-Experience and skills: Cold water surfing requires an additional level of experience and skills. Extreme conditions and cold temperatures can affect a surfer's performance and responsiveness in the water. It is important to have a solid surfing experience and be physically and mentally prepared to face the challenges that come with cold water surfing.

77

Adapted surfing.

It is a form of surfing specifically designed for individuals with physical disabilities.

This activity has become increasingly popular worldwide as it provides people with different abilities the opportunity to enjoy the ocean and experience freedom in the water.

There are various adaptations and specialized equipment that make it possible for individuals with physical disabilities to participate in adapted surfing.

One of the key elements is the use of special surfboards.

These boards are designed to provide stability and balance, making it easier for people with disabilities to stand up and ride the waves.

Adapted boards can have different shapes and sizes, depending on the individual needs of each surfer.

In addition to boards, various assistants and devices are used to help people with disabilities participate in adapted surfing.

Some adapted surfers may require the assistance of instructors or volunteers to help them move in the water and get up on the board.

Harnesses and straps are also used to provide additional stability and allow surfers to maintain their position.

Adapted surfing is not limited only to individuals with physical disabilities; it can also include those with visual or hearing impairments.

Specific adaptations have been developed to enable these individuals to enjoy surfing.

For example, longer and more stable surfboards are used, and tactile or visual signals are employed to guide visually impaired surfers during their water experience.

In addition to being a recreational activity, adapted surfing can also have therapeutic benefits.

The contact with water and the sensation of riding the waves can improve muscle strength, coordination, and balance for individuals with disabilities.

It can also promote self-confidence and the overcoming of physical challenges.

In many places, there are organizations and programs that offer adapted surfing classes and events.

These initiatives aim to foster inclusion and provide opportunities for people with disabilities to enjoy this exciting water activity.

78

Surfing in artificial wave pools.

It is a relatively new way of practicing surfing that has gained popularity in recent years.

These pools are designed to generate controlled and consistent artificial waves, providing surfers with the opportunity to enjoy perfect waves in a controlled environment.

One of the most well-known facilities is the Surf Ranch, created by legendary surfer Kelly Slater in Lemoore, California.

The Surf Ranch utilizes advanced technology to produce high-quality waves in a long rectangular pool.

The system employs a mechanism that displaces water through a series of chambers and sections, creating a wave that travels along the pool.

The largest artificial wave generated at the Surf Ranch is known as "The Beast."

This wave reached a height of nearly 2 meters, making it one of the largest artificial waves ever created.

The wave was designed to provide an exciting and challenging experience for surfers, with a shape and size similar to waves found in the ocean.

The main advantage of surfing in artificial wave pools is the ability to generate waves in a predictable and consistent manner.

Unlike the ocean, where conditions can vary greatly, and quality waves are not always available, artificial wave pools can produce perfect and consistent waves at any time.

This allows surfers to practice and refine their skills more effectively.

Another advantage is the ability to tailor wave conditions to different skill levels.

Artificial wave pools offer the capability to adjust the height, speed, and shape of the waves, allowing experienced surfers to tackle more challenging waves and beginners to enjoy gentler and more accessible waves.

This makes surfing in artificial wave pools appealing to both professionals and enthusiasts.

However, it is important to note that surfing in artificial wave pools also has some limitations and challenges.

These facilities require expensive infrastructure and technology for construction and maintenance, limiting their availability and access.

79

Surfing has been a recurring theme in cinema throughout the decades, both in documentaries exploring surf culture and lifestyle, and in fictional movies that use surfing as a central element of the plot.

Some iconic films about surfing include:

-**"The Endless Summer" (1966):** Directed by Bruce Brown, this documentary follows two surfers on their quest for the best waves around the world. "The Endless Summer" became a classic and helped popularize surfing globally.

-**"Point Break" (1991):** Directed by Kathryn Bigelow, this action film stars Keanu Reeves and Patrick Swayze and tells the story of an undercover FBI agent who infiltrates a gang of surfers suspected of committing robberies. "Point Break" combines surfing, crime, and adrenaline in an exciting plot.

-**"Blue Crush" (2002):** This drama and romance film follows the life of Anne Marie, a young surfer from Hawaii preparing to compete in a major surfing competition. "Blue Crush" showcases the dedication and passion of a surfer as she faces personal challenges and seeks success in the sport.

-**"Chasing Mavericks" (2012):** Based on the real-life story of surfer Jay Moriarity, played by Gerard Butler, this film narrates the journey of a young surfer in search of the legendary Mavericks wave, one of the biggest and most dangerous in the world. "Chasing Mavericks" is an inspiring tale of personal growth and courage in the world of surfing.

-**"Soul Surfer" (2011):** Based on the true story of Bethany Hamilton, this film follows the life of a young surfer who loses an arm in a shark attack and her struggle to get back in the water and compete again. "Soul Surfer" is a heartwarming story of resilience and determination.

80

The world record for simultaneous surfing.

It is an impressive achievement where a large number of surfers gather to ride the same wave at the same time.

The record was set on February 14, 2015, at the famous Bondi Beach in Sydney, Australia.

On that day, 320 surfers managed to stand up and surf together on a single wave, breaking the previous record set in 2009 in South Africa, where 110 surfers simultaneously rode waves.

The event at Bondi Beach was organized by the Australian surfboard company "The Board Meeting" in collaboration with SurfAid, a charitable organization working to improve the health and well-being of coastal communities.

The main objective of these simultaneous surfing records is not only to set a mark but also to bring the surfing community together and raise funds for charitable causes related to the sport and the marine environment.

Additionally, events like these help promote surfing and raise awareness about its significance in coastal culture and lifestyle.

It's important to note that this record is specific to a particular wave and doesn't necessarily represent the highest number of people surfing simultaneously on different waves in a given location.

In massive simultaneous surfing events like the one held at Bondi Beach, meticulous organization is required to ensure the participants' safety and prevent collisions or other incidents.

81

Aerial surfing.

It is a discipline in surfing characterized by performing maneuvers and tricks in the air while riding a wave.

This technique requires skill, balance, and physical strength, adding a spectacular element to traditional surfing.

Aerial maneuvers in surfing involve taking off from the wave's surface and performing different acrobatics in the air before landing back on the wave.

Some of the most common tricks in aerial surfing include:

- **Aerials:** This involves performing a jump where the surfer takes off from the wave and elevates in the air before landing again. During the jump, turns, rotations, and other acrobatics can be performed to add style and difficulty.

- **Rodeos:** In this maneuver, the surfer rotates in the air while performing a jump. They can complete a full rotation or even multiple rotations before landing on the wave.

- **360s:** This involves performing a full rotation in the air, spinning 360 degrees before landing. This maneuver requires good control and coordination to achieve a smooth rotation and land on the wave correctly.

- **Flip tricks:** These are tricks where the surfer performs a somersault or full spin in the air before landing. These tricks are usually more advanced and require greater skill and strength.

Aerial surfing has become very popular in modern surfing, especially among professional surfers and competitors in high-level events.

Aerial maneuvers bring a unique and creative style to surfing and have influenced the evolution and progression of the sport.

Additionally, aerial surfing has been facilitated by the design and development of surfboards specifically for these types of maneuvers.

Aerial surfboards often have shorter lengths, lower volume, and special fins that allow for greater control and maneuverability in the air.

Aerial surfing not only requires technical skill but also a good read of the wave and the right timing to take off at the precise moment.

Surfers who master this technique can create moments of great spectacle and artistic expression in the water.

82

Eddie Aikau.

He was a prominent Hawaiian surfer and rescuer who became a legend in the surfing community.

He was born on May 4, 1946, in Maui, Hawaii, and grew up on the island of Oahu, where he developed his passion for the ocean and surfing.

Eddie Aikau was known for his exceptional ability to ride big waves, especially at the famous Waimea Bay beach on the north shore of Oahu.

He was one of the first surfers to challenge and master the massive and dangerous waves of Waimea Bay, setting a standard of bravery and skill in big wave surfing.

In addition to his surfing prowess, Eddie Aikau stood out for his dedication and spirit of service as a rescuer.

In 1968, he became the first professional lifeguard hired to patrol the beaches of the north shore of Oahu.

Eddie had an exceptional ability to face extreme conditions and rescue people in danger in the ocean.

The most famous incident associated with Eddie Aikau occurred in 1978 when the surf competition "Quiksilver in Memory of Eddie Aikau" was scheduled to take place at Waimea Bay, but the waves were so massive and dangerous that the competition was canceled.

Eddie, concerned for the safety of the surfers, volunteered to paddle out to sea in search of help after the canoe he was on sank.

Unfortunately, Eddie Aikau was never found.

It is presumed that he was lost at sea while seeking help for his companions.

His disappearance left a profound impact on the surfing community in Hawaii and around the world.

Eddie Aikau personified the spirit of aloha, courage, and sacrifice in his passion for surfing and rescue.

In his honor, the annual surf event "Quiksilver in Memory of Eddie Aikau" was established, which takes place at Waimea Bay when the waves reach a minimum height of 20 feet (approximately 6 meters).

83

Bethany Hamilton is an American professional surfer born on February 8, 1990, in Lihue, Hawaii.

At the age of 13, on October 31, 2003, while surfing in her hometown of Kauai, she was attacked by a tiger shark approximately 4 meters long.

The attack resulted in the amputation of her left arm at the shoulder.

Despite the tragedy, Bethany refused to give up her passion for surfing.

Incredibly, just one month after the attack, she returned to the water and continued surfing.

Using a modified surfboard with a special strap to secure her body and adapted techniques, Bethany demonstrated astonishing determination and personal resilience.

Bethany's comeback to surfing was inspiring and captured the attention of media worldwide.

Her story of resilience and courage became a symbol of overcoming adversity and motivation for many people facing similar challenges.

After her return, Bethany Hamilton continued to compete in professional surf competitions.

She won several championships and became one of the most recognized and respected surfers globally.

Her story was brought to the big screen in 2011 with the movie "Soul Surfer," starring AnnaSophia Robb as Bethany.

In addition to her career as a surfer, Bethany is also a motivational speaker and author.

She has written several books, including her memoir titled "Soul Surfer: A True Story of Faith, Family, and Fighting to Get Back on the Board."

Over the years, Bethany Hamilton has continued to inspire millions of people with her story of overcoming adversity and her positive attitude toward life.

Her dedication to surfing and indomitable spirit has left a lasting impact on the surfing community and beyond.

84

Shane Dorian's feat of riding the "wave of the century" at Mavericks, California, in 1998 is considered a milestone in the history of surfing.

Mavericks is a famous beach located near Half Moon Bay in Northern California, known for its massive waves that form due to specific ocean and seafloor conditions.

At times, the waves at Mavericks can reach extraordinary heights and pose a challenge for surfers.

On December 28, 1994, a photograph taken by Frank Quirarte captured a massive, unnamed wave at Mavericks, which sparked interest among surfers to challenge those extreme conditions.

In the following years, Mavericks became a benchmark for daring surfers seeking thrills and extreme challenges.

On January 23, 1998, a massive swell approached Mavericks and created one of the largest waves ever recorded at that location.

The wave was estimated to be over 18 meters (60 feet) tall, making it one of the biggest waves ever surfed in history.

It was on that epic day that Shane Dorian, a renowned Hawaiian surfer, decided to face the challenge and ride the "wave of the century."

Dorian, known for his bravery and outstanding skills in extreme conditions, successfully rode and navigated that enormous wave in a spectacular manner.

Shane Dorian's feat at Mavericks became a milestone in the world of surfing.

85

The world of surfing features a series of iconic events that bring together the best surfers in the world and attract the attention of the global surfing community.

These standout events take place in different locations around the world and are considered some of the most important on the surfing calendar.

Some of the most famous events in the world of surfing are:

- **World Surf League (WSL):** The World Surf League is the leading organization overseeing and sanctioning professional surfing events worldwide. The WSL organizes various championships and circuits, including the Championship Tour (CT), which is the highest category of professional competition. CT events are held in different locations around the world, such as Australia, Brazil, Hawaii, Indonesia, South Africa, among others.

- **Pipeline Masters:** Held at the famous Pipeline wave on the island of Oahu, Hawaii, this event is one of the most prestigious in the world of surfing. It is part of the WSL's CT and takes place annually in December. Pipeline is known for its perfect and challenging barrels, and surfers compete to conquer this legendary wave.

- **Teahupo'o:** Located in Tahiti, French Polynesia, Teahupo'o is known for having some of the biggest and most dangerous waves in the world. The event at Teahupo'o is part of the CT and is renowned for its impressive barrels and the sheer power of the waves. Surfers face extreme conditions and perform daring maneuvers in pursuit of victory.

- **Uluwatu:** Situated in Bali, Indonesia, Uluwatu is a famous surf spot and hosts a significant event on the CT. The wave at Uluwatu is known for its beauty and consistency, offering long barrels and fast sections. The event attracts surfers from around the world who compete for the title and glory at this iconic Balinese wave.

- **Margaret River Pro:** Held in Margaret River, Western Australia, this event is part of the WSL's CT. Margaret River is known for its powerful and challenging waves, attracting the world's top surfers. The event takes place in April and offers a mix of high-quality waves and challenging conditions.

86

The oldest known surfboard.

The oldest surfboard ever found to date was discovered in 1905 during an archaeological excavation in Huanchaco, a coastal town near Trujillo on the northern coast of Peru.

The surfboard, known as the "Huanchaco Reedboard," was found in a tomb and is estimated to be over 5,000 years old.

The Huanchaco Reedboard is made of balsa wood, a lightweight and buoyant material that was abundant in the region.

It has an elongated and narrow shape, with an approximate length of 1.5 meters (5 feet).

Although it has suffered damage and deterioration over time, the manufacturing and design details can still be appreciated.

This archaeological discovery has provided concrete evidence that the practice of surfing dates back to a much earlier time than previously thought.

Prior to the discovery of the Huanchaco Reedboard, it was believed that surfing originated in the Hawaiian Islands, where it developed over centuries.

The finding of the Huanchaco surfboard has led to a reconsideration of the history and origins of surfing.

It demonstrates that pre-Columbian cultures along the coastal region of Peru were already practicing surfing thousands of years ago, using wooden boards to ride the waves.

Huanchaco, the place where the Huanchaco Reedboard was found, has become a popular destination for surfers seeking to connect with the history and tradition of surfing.

The area boasts a rich surfing culture and has become a landmark for those interested in exploring the origins of this ancient sport.

The Huanchaco Reedboard is an important testament to the history of surfing and its evolution over time.

It also highlights the deep connection that humans have had with the ocean and waves for millennia, demonstrating that the love and passion for surfing transcend barriers of time and geography.

87

The highest speed record achieved on a surfboard.

On November 21, 2017, Matt Wilkinson, a professional surfer from Australia, achieved an impressive top speed on a surfboard.

It happened during a surfing session at Lennox Head, a famous beach in New South Wales, Australia.

While riding a wave at Lennox Head, Wilkinson used his skill and expertise to maximize the speed generated by the wave.

During his descent, he was timed and reached a maximum speed of 62.34 kilometers per hour (38.78 miles per hour).

This milestone in surf speed is remarkable and demonstrates the incredible ability of professional surfers to harness the energy of waves and reach astonishing speeds.

Wilkinson's speed at Lennox Head set a new record at that time and became a benchmark in the world of surfing.

88

The Bay of Fundy, located on the eastern coast of Canada between the provinces of Nova Scotia and New Brunswick, is known for having the highest tides in the world.

The Bay of Fundy is characterized by its funnel shape and unique geography, which contribute to the amplification of tides.

The bay's shape, combined with the natural resonance of the water in the Gulf of Maine, creates a significant increase in tide amplitude.

The tidal range in the Bay of Fundy can vary, but on average, the difference in height between low and high tide can exceed 16 meters (52 feet).

This means that the water can rise and fall considerably in a short period of time.

This phenomenon of extreme tides creates unique and diverse conditions in the Bay of Fundy, attracting surfers and ocean enthusiasts from around the world.

During high tide, powerful waves and currents form, while during low tide, vast areas of sand and unique underwater landscapes are exposed.

Surfing in the Bay of Fundy is challenging and thrilling due to the amplitude and rapidity of the tides.

Surfers must have a deep understanding of currents and tides to be able to enjoy the waves in this area.

In addition to surfing, the Bay of Fundy is famous for its incredible coastal ecosystems and diverse marine life.

It is also home to the iconic Hopewell Rocks, which emerge during low tide and offer a unique experience for visitors.

The Bay of Fundy is a popular tourist destination due to its natural beauty and the unique phenomenon of its tides.

The extreme tides and ever-changing conditions make this bay a special place to explore and enjoy nature in all its splendor.

89

The wetsuit. It is a fundamental garment for surfers and other water sports enthusiasts that allows them to stay warm and protected in cold waters.

The wetsuit was invented by Hugh Bradner, an American physicist and chemist, in 1951.

Bradner worked at the Lawrence Livermore National Laboratory in California, and his goal was to find a solution to keep divers warm during their dives in cold waters.

Neoprene, the main material of the wetsuit, is a synthetic foam made from chloroprene rubber.

Neoprene is characterized by its ability to retain heat and its flexibility, making it ideal for thermal insulation garments in aquatic environments.

The design of the wetsuit consists of several layers.

The outer layer is resistant and durable, while the core is composed of neoprene of varying thicknesses, depending on the water temperature the user will be exposed to. The colder the water, the thicker the neoprene.

The wetsuit works by creating an insulating layer of water between the surfer's body and the outer surface of the suit.

This layer of water is heated by the user's body heat and helps keep them warm during their time in the water.

In addition to providing thermal insulation, the wetsuit also offers protection against scrapes, abrasions, and the ultraviolet radiation from the sun.

Some wetsuits also have strategically placed panels to enhance flexibility and allow for greater range of motion.

The wetsuit has become an essential part of the gear for surfers, divers, and other water sports enthusiasts as it allows them to enjoy their activities for longer periods and in a variety of weather conditions.

Since its invention, the wetsuit has undergone significant technological advancements, such as improvements in design, material quality, and manufacturing techniques.

These advancements have led to the development of lighter, more flexible, and thermally efficient wetsuits.

90

In 2015, young Brazilian surfer Lucas Chianca, nicknamed "Chumbo," achieved a remarkable milestone by becoming the youngest surfer to ride a giant wave in Nazaré, Portugal.

Lucas Chianca, born on May 26, 1999, in Brazil, started his surfing career at a young age and quickly showcased great talent and skill in the water.

At the age of 15, Chianca made history by riding a giant wave in Nazaré, one of the world's most famous locations for surfing massive waves.

Nazaré is known for its unique conditions that generate extraordinarily large waves.

The combination of underwater geography, ocean currents, and weather conditions can produce giant waves that push the limits of what is considered surfable.

In 2015, during one of the surf sessions in Nazaré, Lucas Chianca had the opportunity to face a massive wave and was determined to make the most of it.

With his bravery and skills, he successfully rode the giant wave, thus becoming the youngest surfer to achieve such a feat in that location.

Lucas Chianca's accomplishment caught the attention of the surfing community and earned him recognition and praise for his bravery and expertise in extreme conditions.

His performance in Nazaré opened doors for a professional career in the world of big wave surfing.

Since then, Lucas Chianca has continued to excel in big wave surfing, competing in events and constantly pushing the limits of the sport.

He has won awards and accolades for his performances in the water and has become a prominent figure in the big wave surfing scene.

91

Brazilian surfer Carlos Burle achieved a remarkable feat in 2011 by surfing a giant wave in Nazaré, Portugal, without using a surfboard.

Carlos Burle is known for his bravery and skill in big wave surfing.

During a surf session in Nazaré, a spot renowned for its massive waves, Burle decided to push the conventional limits of the sport and attempt something unprecedented: surfing a wave without a surfboard.

Instead of using a surfboard, Burle was towed by a personal watercraft to the giant wave.

Once on the wave, he let go of the tow rope and relied solely on his body and skill to ride the wave.

This challenging and risky feat required great dexterity and a deep understanding of ocean and wave characteristics.

Burle demonstrated impressive mastery by maintaining balance and harnessing the energy of the wave without the support of a surfboard.

Carlos Burle's achievement captured the attention of the surfing community and earned him international recognition.

His bravery and ability to surf without a board were considered a milestone in the sport and solidified his position as one of the foremost surfers in the realm of big wave surfing.

It's worth noting that surfing without a board is an extremely challenging and dangerous practice.

It requires profound knowledge of the sea, excellent physical fitness, and exceptional water skills.

Only experienced surfers with outstanding abilities should attempt such feats.

92

The world's first surf shop was established in 1949 and was called "The Surf Shop."

It was founded by Dale Velzy, a Californian surfer and entrepreneur, in Manhattan Beach, California.

Dale Velzy is recognized as an important figure in surfing history and is credited with opening the first store specializing in surf-related items.

Prior to the opening of "The Surf Shop," surfers used to make their own boards and obtain other necessary equipment in an improvised manner.

With the opening of "The Surf Shop," Velzy created a place where surfers could buy surfboards, swimwear, and other surf-related accessories.

The shop became a gathering spot for the local surfing community and served as a starting point for the growth of the surf industry.

The location of "The Surf Shop" in Manhattan Beach, California, was strategic due to the excellent surfing conditions in the area and the presence of a vibrant community of surfers.

The store quickly became a popular destination and started attracting surfers from around the world.

The opening of the first surf shop marked the beginning of a growing industry.

As surfing gained popularity, more specialized surf shops emerged worldwide, offering a wide range of products and services for surfers.

Dale Velzy, in addition to being an entrepreneur, was a talented surfboard shaper.

His influence on the development of surfboard design and manufacturing was significant during those early years of surf culture.

The opening of "The Surf Shop" laid the foundation for the growth and expansion of the surf industry.

Since then, surfing has become a global sport, with surf shops found in nearly every place where waves attract sports enthusiasts.

93

The origin of the leash, also known as "amarre" in Spanish, is associated with Californian surfer Pat O'Neill, who is credited with its invention in the 1970s.

Prior to the development of the leash, surfers didn't have an effective way to keep their surfboard close to them after falling off, often resulting in long and exhausting swimming sessions to retrieve the board.

Pat O'Neill, son of legendary surfer and entrepreneur Jack O'Neill, was looking for a solution to avoid constantly swimming to retrieve his board after falling off.

In 1971, O'Neill introduced the leash, an elastic cord that connects to the surfboard at one end and secures to the surfer's ankle at the other end.

The leash was a significant breakthrough in the sport of surfing, as it allowed surfers to stay connected to their boards even after falling off.

This improved both the safety and comfort of surfers, preventing boards from floating freely and potentially hitting other surfers or getting lost at sea.

Pat O'Neill's invention was a game-changer in surfing, as it enabled surfers to have more freedom and confidence to perform riskier maneuvers and surf in more challenging conditions.

The leash quickly became an essential accessory for surfers worldwide.

Since its invention, the leash has undergone improvements and refinements in terms of materials, design, and functionality.

Nowadays, there are different types of leashes that cater to the individual preferences and needs of surfers.

94

Surfing in Antarctica.

Some intrepid surfers have defied the extreme conditions and surfed in Antarctica.

Surfing in Antarctica is an extremely challenging and uncommon activity.

Due to its location at the South Pole, Antarctica is known for having some of the most extreme weather conditions on the planet, with very cold temperatures, strong winds, and icy waters.

The waves in Antarctica are generated by glaciers and tend to be quite different from waves found in other surf regions.

These waves are irregular, powerful, and can be unpredictable due to the natural conditions and unique landscape of Antarctica.

Surfing in Antarctica requires specialized preparation and equipment.

Surfers must wear extremely thick and cold-resistant wetsuits, as well as carry additional safety equipment such as flotation devices and hypothermia protection.

Furthermore, access to Antarctica is complicated and subject to strict regulations and permits.

Most surfers who venture to surf in Antarctica are experts in extreme conditions and have a support team to ensure their safety.

Surfing in Antarctica is considered a niche activity, and only a few dedicated surfers have had the opportunity and courage to face these extreme conditions.

For them, surfing in Antarctica represents a unique challenge and a way to explore and connect with nature in one of the most remote and inhospitable places in the world.

95

Paddleboarding, also known as stand-up paddle surfing (SUP), is a discipline in which surfers use a larger board and paddle to move through the water and catch waves.

Here are some key aspects of paddleboarding:

-Equipment: In paddleboarding, surfers use a specific board called an "SUP board" or "paddleboard." These boards are typically larger, wider, and more stable than conventional surfboards. The paddles used are longer, with a blade at one end that is submerged in the water for paddling. Paddles can be made of various materials, such as carbon fiber or aluminum. -Origins: Paddleboarding has its roots in ancient Polynesian culture, where fishermen used paddleboards to navigate the water. The modern version of SUP gained popularity in the 1960s in Hawaii, where surf instructors started using larger boards and paddles to have a better perspective while teaching students.

-Practice: To engage in paddleboarding, surfers stand on the board and use the paddle to paddle and move through the water. The paddle is used for balance and propulsion. Surfers can paddle on flatwater, such as lakes or rivers, or seek out waves to ride. -Physical Benefits: Paddleboarding is a complete exercise that engages multiple muscle groups, including the arms, legs, abs, and back. Paddling strengthens the upper body muscles, improves balance and coordination, and also provides a good cardiovascular workout.

-Modalities: In addition to wave paddleboarding, there are other SUP modalities. Flatwater paddling is a popular form of exercise and recreation, where surfers can paddle along the coastline, explore rivers or lakes, or even participate in paddleboard races. There are also disciplines like SUP yoga, where yoga poses are performed on the board, and SUP fitness, which combines fitness exercises on the board.

96

The city of Huanchaco, Peru, was recognized as the "City of Surfing" by the Peruvian government in 2017.

Huanchaco is famous for its consistent waves and rich surfing history.

–Location: Huanchaco is a small coastal city located in the La Libertad region in northern Peru. It is approximately 12 kilometers north of the city of Trujillo, a major city in the region.

–Waves and Conditions: Huanchaco is known for its consistent waves and is considered a renowned surfing destination in Peru. The sea conditions in Huanchaco are ideal for surfing year-round. The waves are suitable for both beginners and more experienced surfers.

–Caballitos de Totora Boards: A unique feature of surfing in Huanchaco is the use of traditional boards called "Caballitos de Totora." These boards are handcrafted from totora, a local aquatic plant. Caballitos de Totora have been used in Huanchaco for centuries and are considered part of the city's cultural heritage.

–History of Surfing in Huanchaco: Huanchaco has a long history in the world of surfing. It is said that surfing has been practiced in the region for over 3,000 years, making it one of the oldest surf spots in the world. Local fishermen in Huanchaco used caballitos de totora to navigate and fish in the sea, which later transformed into a form of entertainment and sport.

–Competitions and Events: Huanchaco has hosted numerous national and international surfing competitions. The recognition of the city as the "City of Surfing" has boosted tourism and the organization of surf-related events. These events attract surfers from different parts of the world and contribute to the local economy.

–Surf Schools and Surf Culture: Huanchaco has several surf schools where visitors can learn to surf or improve their skills in the water. The surf culture is deeply rooted in the city, with surf shops, restaurants, and accommodations catering to surfers and tourists interested in the sport.

97

Dolphin surfing is an incredibly special and exciting experience for fortunate surfers who have the opportunity to witness it.

–Dolphin Encounters: During surf sessions, surfers may occasionally encounter dolphins in the water. Dolphins are known to be curious and social, and they sometimes approach surfers. These encounters can happen in different locations around the world, both in oceanic waters and more sheltered coastlines.

–Dolphin Behavior: Dolphins often swim and play in groups called "pods" or "schools." They are intelligent and agile animals, and they are often attracted to the waves and energy created by surfers in the water. They can swim alongside surfers, leap and perform acrobatics, providing a fascinating and joyful spectacle.

–Magical Experience: Surfing with dolphins is considered a magical and enriching experience. Seeing these magnificent marine mammals in their natural habitat, sharing moments in the water while surfing, creates a special connection with nature and brings a sense of awe and joy.

–Emotional Benefits: The presence of dolphins in the water can evoke positive emotions and a sense of calmness and happiness. Interacting with these charismatic and playful animals can be therapeutic and uplift the spirits of surfers. Many describe dolphin surfing as an inspiring and transformative experience.

–Care and Respect: It is essential to remember that dolphins are wild and protected animals. When encountering them in the water, it is important to maintain a safe distance and respect their space. Attempting to touch or disturb their natural behavior should be avoided. Observing them from afar and enjoying their company responsibly is the best way to interact with them.

–Connection with the Ocean: Dolphin surfing can also help foster greater awareness and connection with the ocean. These animals are integral parts of the marine ecosystem, and their presence highlights the importance of protecting and conserving the oceans and marine life.

98

Miki Dora, born in 1934, is recognized as one of the first surfers to make a living through surfing.

–Style and Attitude: He was known for his fluid style and rebellious attitude in the water. His surfing style was characterized by smooth and elegant movements on the waves, earning him the nickname "Da Cat." Dora stood out for his ability to glide effortlessly on the waves.

–Influence on Surf Culture: He became an iconic figure in the 1960s surf culture. His style and attitude influenced a generation of surfers and became a role model for many. His carefree approach and passion for surfing made him a legendary figure in the surfing community.

–Leadership in the "Malibu Mafia" Movement: He was part of the group known as the "Malibu Mafia" in the 1960s, which included other prominent surfers from Malibu, California. This group was influential in shaping surf culture and establishing a unique lifestyle associated with surfing.

–Professional Career: He was one of the first surfers to earn money through sponsorships and competitions. Although he refused to participate in formal contests, he leveraged his fame and skills to appear in surf movies, perform exhibitions, and participate in promotional events. He also worked as a model and actor in the film industry.

–Controversies and Legacy: Despite his surfing success, Miki Dora was involved in several controversies throughout his life. He was known for his rebellious nature and disregard for established norms. His attitude and actions often generated mixed opinions within the surfing community.

99

Submarine surfing, also known as underwater surfing or underwater bodyboarding, is a form of surfing that is practiced beneath the water's surface instead of on the surface.

-Equipment: Submarine surfers use scuba diving equipment such as wetsuits, fins, masks, and snorkels. These items allow them to submerge and stay underwater for extended periods of time.

-Boards: Unlike conventional surfboards, the boards used in submarine surfing are typically shorter and more rigid. They are designed to maneuver and glide beneath the water's surface.

-Locations: Submarine surfers seek out locations with reefs or underwater breakers where waves break beneath the water. These spots can be found in different parts of the world, such as Hawaii, Tahiti, and the Maldives.

-Techniques: Submarine surfers employ special techniques to glide beneath the water and ride underwater waves. They can swim beneath the wave and ride along the seabed or maneuver around reefs and underwater formations.

-Risks and Precautions: Like any form of surfing, submarine surfing also involves certain risks. Surfers must be familiar with the marine environment, be aware of currents, and ensure they have the appropriate safety equipment. It is also important to have adequate diving and breath-holding skills, as good lung capacity and efficient breathing techniques are required.

-Filming and Photography: Submarine surfing has also sparked interest in the realm of underwater filming and photography. Special cameras and accessories have been created to capture the exhilarating images of surfers while they ride beneath the water.

100

Desert surfing is a unique way to practice this sport as it takes place in arid and remote locations, far from the coastlines.

While it may seem surprising, there are certain geographical and climatic conditions that allow for the formation of waves in the middle of the desert, providing surfers with an unusual yet thrilling experience.

–Namib Desert (Namibia): Located on the southwestern coast of Africa, it is famous for its red sand dunes and spectacular landscapes. Along the coast, where the desert meets the Atlantic Ocean, unique conditions arise that generate sand waves. The wind blowing from the sea collides with the dunes, creating ripples in the sand that resemble ocean waves. Surfers take advantage of these formations to glide over the dunes using special sandboards or even modified surfboards.

–Atacama Desert (Chile): Considered one of the driest places on Earth, it also offers opportunities for desert surfing. Off the coast of Chile, near the city of Iquique, lies the famous wave known as "La ola de la Hija" (The Daughter's Wave), which forms on an extensive sand dune facing the sea. This wave is globally recognized for its size and shape, attracting surfers from around the world seeking a unique desert experience.

–Other Locations: Besides Namibia and Chile, there are other places in the world where desert surfing is practiced. Some examples include the Sahara Desert in Morocco, the Mojave Desert in the United States, and the Rub' al Khali Desert in Saudi Arabia. These locations also feature sand dune formations and favorable conditions for the creation of sand waves. It is important to note that desert surfing significantly differs from ocean surfing, as sand waves are less predictable and may require specific skills and equipment. Surfers typically use wider boards with fewer fins to adapt to the sandy conditions.

101

The world record for the longest surf on a single wave was set by Spanish surfer Antonio Laureiro on September 28, 2019, at La Gravière Beach in Hossegor, France.

During this impressive feat, Antonio Laureiro surfed a single wave for 8 hours and 15 minutes.

During that record-breaking time, Laureiro covered an astonishing distance of over 37 kilometers (23 miles) on the same wave.

This incredible achievement showcases the physical and mental endurance required to maintain balance and control on a wave for such an extended period.

La Gravière Beach is renowned for its powerful waves and its reputation among experienced surfers.

It is a recognized surf spot in the Hossegor region of southwestern France, attracting surfers from around the world due to its excellent conditions.

If you have enjoyed exploring the wonders and curiosities of the world of surfing presented in this book, we would love to ask you to share your experience and write a review on Amazon.

Your opinion is of great value to us and to other surfing enthusiasts who are looking to discover and learn more about this exciting water sport.

We understand that leaving a review requires a few minutes of your time, but we encourage you to share your thoughts and opinions with us.

Your support is crucial in continuing to provide quality content, as well as tips and fascinating facts about surfing for all the lovers of this sport.

We sincerely appreciate your support and hope that you have enjoyed reading the captivating stories, surfers' achievements, and surprising curiosities we have shared in this book.

Thank you for sharing your experience with us, and we wish you many perfect and thrilling waves in your future surfing sessions!

Printed in Great Britain
by Amazon